SURVIVING THE LEAVING CERT:

Points for
PARENTS

Marie Murray

VERITAS

Published 2002 by
Veritas Publications
7/8 Lower Abbey Street
Dublin 1
Ireland
Email publications@veritas.ie
Website www.veritas.ie

ISBN 1 85390 646 8

Cover design by Pierce Design
Book design by Colette Dower
Typeset by Niamh McGarry
Printed in the Republic of Ireland by Paceprint Ltd, Dublin

*Veritas books are printed on paper made from the wood pulp of
managed forests. For every tree felled, at least one tree is planted,
thereby renewing natural resources.*

This book is dedicated to my daughters,
Karen Murray and Aisling Murray,
for their love and support and for providing me with the
personal experience of parenting Leaving Cert. students.

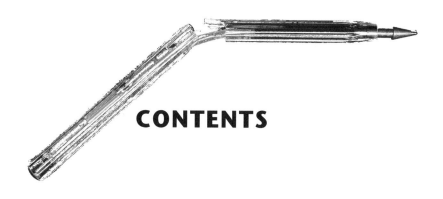

CONTENTS

ACKNOWLEDGEMENTS

There are many people to thank for this book. The staff of St Vincent's Hospital, Fairview always encourage and support me in every professional endeavour, especially Dr Jim O'Boyle, Ned Byrne, Tom Houlihan and fellow psychologist Maeve Kenny. Special gratitude to Eimear Burke, Librarian at St Vincent's, for her genius in finding any article a researcher requires. Colleagues at St Joseph's Adolescent and Family Services are always supportive, thanks to Tom Breen, Kay Burke and all the staff. Especial thanks are extended to the young St Joseph's clients with whom I have worked over the years. They have helped me understand many aspects of their adolescent world.

Acknowledgement must also be made of colleagues and friends in the Department of Psychology, UCD and Trinity College, Dublin and The Psychological Society of Ireland. Thanks also to my fellow faculty members on the new Master's in Systemic Family Therapy at the Department of Education and Professional Studies, University of Limerick; Evelyn Gordon, Declan Roche, Sile Roche and associate member Elizabeth O'Neill.

I am particularly grateful to Anne Carpenter, Department of Humanities, Carlow I.T., for sharing her expertise in education and her research results on first year college students and non-completion. Also, for generously providing me with many textbooks on education.

There were many students at Second and Third Level who shared their views on school life with me. I particularly thank my young advisors, Peter O'Boyle, who first suggested I write this book, Lisa Deignan, and David Neary who helped with the research throughout the past year.

I appreciate many friends and colleagues in *The Irish Times*, especially Rose Doyle, Catherine Foley and Kathryn Holmquist who have pushed me to write about psychology. I am grateful to them for their support. Roslyn Dee in *The Sunday Tribune*, and Mary O'Sullivan in *The Sunday Independent* have also invited me to write articles on adolescent concerns. The *Today with Pat Kenny* team in RTÉ Radio One have provided me with a platform for communicating psychological views to an important listening audience for which I thank Pat Kenny, Series Producer Marian Richardson and the entire team for their warmth and good humour each Thursday when we meet. I am exceptionally grateful to many listeners who have sent messages of encouragement and appreciation.

Finally, my thanks to Veritas Publishers, especially Maura Hyland, Toner Quinn and my editor Helen Carr, for their professionalism at every step of the publication process.

Of course no endeavour has meaning without the loving support of family. Thank you for tolerating my 'absence' during the writing of this book.

Marie Murray

1

UNDERSTANDING THE LEAVING CERT.

The Leaving Cert. has taken on huge significance in Irish society because it is seen as the gateway to success in life. It is the pinnacle of secondary school accomplishment, the ultimate marker of achievement. It purports to predict who will survive, who will succeed and who will achieve in the academic adult world and in the world of work.

One might ask how one exam could become the culmination of an entire educational system. How it could possibly provide conclusive measurement of a young person's potential and access to other educational or vocational worlds? How can the number of Leaving Cert. 'points' a student possesses provide the definitive measurement of a person on school completion?

One answer to this question is that educational qualifications have become the most important currency in Irish society, with high local value and easy foreign exchange. The ultimate 'gift' that many parents seek to present to their children is the gift of education. This has, in many instances, superseded the inheritance of the farm, the family business or the 'promise' of a living on the land. Somehow, 'educational credentials have become the major determinants of wealth, status and power.'[1]

Another answer to the question about how the Leaving Cert. has gained such significance is that its importance derives precisely from its role in determining entry into third-level education, its acceptance as a reflection of intellectual prowess, its apparent capacity to assist or thwart vocational choice and its requirement as a qualification for the world of work.

However, those who have watched the nature, tone and thrust of education change from contemplation to competition, from development of the person to possession of points or from the 'lit fire' to the 'bucket full of facts' might suggest yet another answer. They might say that the Leaving Cert. has become too narrow in what it defines as intelligence, in what it validates as achievement and in what it depicts as success. That the resulting emphasis on performance in examinations and gaining points may take precedence over education. And that these changes in the significance of the Leaving Cert. have taken place in the past three decades as Leaving Cert. grades have become increasingly and inextricably linked to application to University and other Third-Level Educational Institutes.

A further concern about the extraordinary significance of the Leaving Cert. is that there are significant talents, different abilities and alternative intelligences that may be excluded under the current system. It is restrictive to measure thousands of people using primarily one method of measurement, the time-limited, written examination. The inclusion of an understanding of multiple intelligences rather than a singular 'intelligence' is required and the system should, therefore, broaden to include multi-modal methods of multiple intelligence measurement.

Historical Perspectives

In the past it was a privileged minority who could remain in full-time education into Secondary School and up to Leaving Cert. Entrance to college was available to an even smaller number who could afford it. The transition out of childhood and into the world of work frequently took place at the age of fourteen, compulsory school attendance up to that age having been introduced in Ireland in 1927.

People who left school aged fourteen had usually completed primary school and had sat what was then called the Primary Cert. This state exam provided a measure of basic educational attainment in English, Irish and Arithmetic and was the sole qualification with which many people went out to work.

Those who had the advantage of entering secondary school were a privileged minority before the introduction of free education in Secondary School in 1967 by former Education Minister Donough O'Malley.

The access to second level provided by 'free education' certainly increased opportunities for those who previously could not even consider secondary school and eased the financial burden on many others.

The abolition of college fees in 1995 by former Education Minister Niamh Bhreathnach, might have been expected to similarly assist the so-called 'disadvantaged' into third level, but in many instances parents had already pushed themselves to the limit keeping their children in second-level education. Free education is rarely free, it denied an income that would have been available had the student left school and worked. It required investment in books and uniforms and commodities that no allowance could cover sufficiently. The so-called 'voluntary contributions' asked for by schools created a divide between those who could or could not afford it. To be fair, it was sometimes a psychological divide. But even so, it also often created a sense of inferiority in the family could not pay its way.

Additionally, as large numbers took up the option of second level to Leaving Cert, minimum educational requirements for jobs increased in tandem, thereby making secondary school credentials necessary for basic employment that previously accepted a Primary Cert. or Intermediate Cert.[2]

There was also, of course, an increase in demand for third-level places. The abolition of college fees did, indeed, provide access to education for some people previously denied this privilege, although there has been public debate about this (see Clifford, M. 2002). The demographics in society in the past ten years have also been of a disproportionately young population who now had second-level qualifications and were considering third-level. This in turn, however, has lead to levels of competition for places that have required increasing the academic criteria for entry to oversubscribed courses. There has followed a series of moves and countermoves by students to circumvent these requirements, by repeating the Leaving Cert., attending grinds and subject courses, undertaking summer tuition and strategising towards the acquisition of points, sometimes at the expense of a broader education.

The solution to this does not lie in increasing college registration fees to the point where they become as high as actual fees; an erosion of the benefit within a short seven years. The reported statement by the current Minister for Education,[3] Noel Dempsey that 'if underprivileged students would be best served by reintroduction of fees' he would 'look at the issue' may fail to take account of the fact that underprivilege begins long before third-level and begins in the very construction of 'underprivileged'. It is not by denying money in one quarter, but by examining the system from primary school upwards to determine the factors that invite some people into education and exclude others. This returns the debate full circle to *what is intelligence?, who decides?, how do we measure it? and what place is there within our educational system for more recognition of multiple intelligence from the earliest educational encounter by the child?* That would, perhaps, warrant much more debate that this introduction can provide.

However, to deal with the possible and the present, there has been excellent examination of the Leaving Cert. stage and the qualities and inequalities that may obtain in the points system carried out by the Commission on the Points System. This now requires some discussion.

Commission on Points System

Such has been the concern about the points system that a Commission was set up by former Minister for Education and

Science, Michael Martin, in October 1997 to examine the system of selection for third-level entry in this country. This recognised that, while it was important to ensure a transparent, impartial and efficient system for entry to third-level institutions, the system should be reviewed for the following:

- Effect on the personal development of students.
- Influence on teaching, learning and assessment techniques.
- Impact on selection of third-level courses.
- Effect on access to third-level for educationally disadvantaged students.
- Effect on access to third-level for mature students.

Educational Ideas

There are a number of ideas, which have influenced debates about education, that are worth discussing because of the part they play in how parents and students might understand the Leaving Cert. process that they are about to embark on.

Sheelagh Drudy and Kathleen Lynch, in a sociological study of schools and society in Ireland (1993), identify three of the most prominent ideas that influence Irish education as follows:[4]

1 The first of these is a particular idea of society itself called *consensualism*. This assumes that there is consensus or agreement in a society. For example, that there is consensus about what is meant by the term 'disadvantage'. However, the definition of disadvantage is usually decided by those who are *not* disadvantaged. This has allowed educationalists to interpret lack of educational progress amongst certain groups as deriving from their social class or 'disadvantage' rather than arising from the educational system itself.

2 The second dominant idea in education concerns what is called *essentialism*. Essentialism focuses on the individual as exclusively responsible for their achievement. It defines the

person as having a certain fixed and limited ability. The problem with essentialism is that it can conveniently locate the problem of attainment in the individual and *not* in the educational system that measures attainment in limited ways. This way of thinking contributes to the narrow definition of intelligence, which dismisses many other forms of intelligence[5] as irrelevant or invalid.

3 The third dominant idea in Irish education concerns the relationship of the individual to society called *meritocracy*. Essentially this is the principle by which merit is regarded as the combination of *ability plus effort*. Those with ability who put in the effort will be rewarded, thus creating equal opportunity for all. However, as Drudy and Lynch point out[6] this makes those who fail feel 'that they lack some vital human ability (such as IQ) required in society'. It makes them feel that it is their own fault for not trying hard enough.

These three dominant ideas and approaches to education are part of what has brought about *credentialism*, which is the acquisition of more and more credited qualifications. This turns learning into a commodity and puts people into a competitive race to acquire more and more credential currency as a means of accessing financial reward, social power and status.

The Experience of Students

The Leaving Cert. occurs at a critical developmental time in a young person's life. There are many other important tasks, goals, worries and concerns going on in the life of the Leaving Cert. student that frequently do not even get discussed during the Leaving Cert. year.

Students entering their Leaving Cert. year and contemplating completing the Central Applications Office (CAO) forms for third-level places may become distressed and burdened by what seem to be the overwhelming tasks of their age and life stage. The cultural primacy of the Leaving Cert. can make the task daunting to young people already in the throes of many changes in their adolescent lives. Many students speak about how difficult it is to have to make choices for the future based on estimates of how one will perform in an exam that is to be taken later in the year. There are students who have likened this procedure to laying odds in the Grand National.

Indeed, it is a Grand National of a different kind. One has to know how many people are sitting the exam, the courses that are most popular in any particular year, the number of places on these courses, the likelihood of the points required for the courses going up or down in that particular exam year, and finally the likelihood of the student's own personal achievement. This is akin to laying odds, estimating the number of runners, the number of places and the probability of being a winner.

Furthermore, the finishing post can be changed from one event to the next and while the race itself is in progress, as witnessed in the significant increases and decreases in points requirements in the first round of CAO offers this year, 2002.

Gateway to the Future

If the Leaving Cert. is a gateway to success it is a narrow one. Too narrow, perhaps, for all who seek to pass through it in the annual rush for points and privileged places. Too narrow to facilitate those who learn differently.

Because it is a narrow gateway there are students who get emotionally pushed and shoved, battered and bruised and trampled upon. There are psychological injuries to self-esteem and to confidence. More seriously, there may be significant injuries to adolescent identity.

Leaving Certificate Points Race

The Leaving Certificate has become a race for points and a number of negative factors are associated with the system. The Points Commission Report[7] confirms some of the damaging effects that might be attributed to the points system as follows:

Negative Aspect of Points System

- Negative impact on students' personal development.
- Subject choices made by students may be influenced by the need to attain the highest level of points for third-level entry rather than being chosen because of interest or educational value.
- The danger of a narrowing of the curriculum.
- Undue focus on the attainment of examination results.
- Problems in the variation in grading between subjects in the Leaving Cert.
- The once-off nature of the exam.
- The media focus on a small number of courses with very high points requirements.
- The ESRI study's findings of much higher levels of stress amongst Junior and Leaving Certificate examination students than among young adults or older people, which seem to arise from the pressure to succeed.
- The neglect of non-academic activities than among young adults or older people.

Positive Recommendations to Points Commission[8]

However, the report also highlights the many recommendations submitted to the commission and the relevance of some of those ideas as follows:

- Recognition that a broader range of achievements should be recognised.[9]
- That a much wider range of intelligences and achievements should be included in the assessment. These were expanded

out to include *'observation, problem identification, problem solving, reasoning, taking initiative and responsibility for learning'*.

- This is consistent with Howard Gardner's[10] Multiple Intelligences Theory, which broadens what we consider intelligence to be to include a whole range of talents such as visual spatial skills, bodily-kinesthetic abilities, musical talent, interpersonal and intrapersonal skills as well as Linguistic and Logical-Mathematical talents.
- This would, presumably, also include emotional intelligence.[11]
- Other abilities to be considered are the capacity of the student to work in a cooperative way and to have what is described as a sense of social solidarity.
- Also for consideration is the possibility of students sitting different elements of a subject at different times during the two-year senior cycle.
- Greater use of coursework, projects, orals, practical work and fieldwork such as occurs in many other educational systems abroad has been suggested.
- Portfolio Assessment was recommended.
- Most importantly that the commission consider not continuing with a system that is unique to Ireland in relying on 'a single final examination in a single sitting, at a single point in time using a single test instrument'.

While many difficulties arise in the points system it is undeniably a transparent system, which attempts to be equitable, ethical and efficient. Furthermore, until such time as recommendations about the broadening of subjects and the extension of evaluation techniques may be implemented it is the system with which parents and students must now engage.

Conclusion

As parents and students embark on the Leaving Cert. year the chapters in this book are designed as a guide through that process. The challenge for parents and students will be to keep a balance and perspective in the year ahead. To do this it is important that parents and students remain in good relationship with each other. That they can give and receive help along the way. That they can observe when the other person needs space or needs reassurance. That their expectations of each other are realistic, and that success at the end of the year is not just measured in Leaving Cert. 'points'.

Knowledge in every discipline is now greater than any one person can ever possess. Information is available from multiple sources if we know how to access them and use them wisely. The future will not be about rote memory, but about using what one knows well and knowing where and how to find out what one does not know. It will be about discriminating the important from the trivial and learning to funnel mentally the deluges of superficiality, while retaining the nuggets of knowledge that will advance understanding and reflection. It will be about deciding where one stands on issues, what ethical position one holds and how to find a foothold in the various avalanches of ideologies.

More importantly, when anxieties arise about the Leaving Cert. parents and students might remember that we live in a time of opportunities, multiple career paths and myriad ways to get to a chosen career. The Leaving Cert. exam is but one of the markers and signposts on the way.

There is something for everyone and everyone has some talent that is valuable in the world.

Most importantly that parents and students will remember that examinations are just one measure of one aspect of a person. The true value of a person is not measured in points.

Notes

1 Drudy, S. & Lynch, K. (1993) *Schools and Society in Ireland,* Gill and Macmillan, Dublin.
2 Second level exam that was taken in fourth year in secondary school, abolished in favour of Junior Cert in 3rd year.
3 Front page of *The Sunday Business Post,* August 18, 2002.
4 Previously cited. Note 1 above.
5 Gardner H. (1985) *Frames of Mind: The Theory of Multiple Intelligences,* Basic Books, New York. Also Gardner, H. (1993) *Creating Minds,* Basic Books, New York.
6 For full account readers are referred to Drudy, S. & Lynch, K. (1993) *Schools and Society in Ireland,* Gill and Macmillan, Dublin.
7 Commission on the Points System, Final Report 1999.
8 The author acknowledges the sources of this information in the report by Aine Hyland, Chairperson of the Commission on the Point System and the Final Commission Report.
9 The LCVP, Leaving Cert. Vocational Programme, expanded in 1994 and the LCA, Leaving Cert. Applied, introduced in 1995 both recognise a broader range of talents than the traditional Leaving Cert.
10 Previously cited. See note 5 above.
11 Goleman, D. (1996) *Emotional Intelligence: Why it can matter more than IQ,* Bloomsbury, Reading.

2

THE LEAVING CERT. STUDENT

The Leaving Cert. comes at a time when there are many other important transitions going on in the life of the student. This adolescent time is an extraordinary life stage. It is 'the best of times and the worst of times' compressed into a few short years. It includes the culmination of the educational journey through secondary school. It encompasses experiences of a wide range of adolescent processes and the actual completion of the adolescent transition into young adulthood.

For most parents it feels like yesterday that their child entered secondary school. What a transition that seemed to be at the time; the end of childhood, the beginning of adolescence. Yet here, in this Leaving Cert. year, there is another ending and another beginning: the end of adolescence and the beginning of young adulthood.

In that relatively short time, between that first day at secondary school and the first day in 6th year, the child has accomplished developmental transitions of cataclysmic proportions. These are so many, so varied and so altering that they are not unlike the child's absolute beginning in this world, when they graduated from baby to toddler, from cradle to cot, from being lifted to sitting to crawling, walking and talking in the space of a few very short years.

Looking back over those years there have been many factors and influences that have shaped their lives so far. What was inherited, what was experienced and what was provided in the surrounding world. In other words, all the biological, the psychological and the social influences.

These are often referred to as the *biopsychosocial factors* that have affected the development of the student as a person from the very first moment. They include genetic and biological make up, gender, physique and appearance, family composition and interactions, the capacity to relate to others and of others to respond, all influenced by the surrounding social, educational and cultural world.

The life story of the person who is now also a Leaving Cert. student can be understood by examining all of these factors.[1]

The Individual Student

The Leaving Cert. student is, therefore, *not* an abstract entity, but a real person who has had their own particular and unique life experiences.

It can be useful for parents to reflect on their own child in this way, and examine the myriad experiences, circumstances, advantages and disadvantages that may have affected their child in the past and that may now influence their child's capacity to cope with the year ahead.

Early Influences

Early influences play their part in shaping the child, the child's experiences of the world, of other people and of his or her place in relation to others. First impressions are indeed important. The child's first impressions of the world lodge in the recesses of his or her mind. While most people have limited access to memories of their own early childhood, those experiences have considerable influence in later life. The student of today has been shaped by the experiences of yesterday, which may include some of the following:

• The circumstances of birth, whether a longed for baby or an unexpected creation and the views of parents and extended family about this.

- Health during pregnancy, prematurity, postmaturity and the labour and birth itself.
- Gender and whether this was important or immaterial to one or both parents or the extended family.
- Early eating, feeding and sleeping patterns and the individual and joint capacity of parents to deal with this early stage.
- Developmental progress, whether milestones were reached on time, the speed with which skills were acquired and whether or not any interventions were necessary.
- The experience of having brothers and sisters.
- The reaction of these other children in the house and the age gap between each child.
- Subsequent relationships with brothers and sisters.

Early Childhood Experiences

Early childhood experiences, particularly child-minding arrangements, can have long-term consequences. Parents will remember how their child responded to the arrangement they made for child-minding at difference stages in the child's life. Also, looking back on these arrangement, whether they think that they were advantageous to the developing person, or otherwise as follows:

- Childcare arrangements, home, crèche, kindergarten, playschool, school and secondary school experiences.
- Other care situations, orphaned, in care, adopted, fostered, and the situations surrounding these circumstances.
- Whether or not there were separations from family. If so whether they were short or extended, the reason for such separations and the child's experience of these.

Personality

Personality used to be described as the 'character' a person had. It was the highly distinctive patterns of behaving, of thinking and feeling that made up an individual person's style of interacting with the world. But that implies that it is 'fixed'. That a person behaves the same way in every situation. Not so.

Most psychologists would now agree that personality is much more interactive than that. Personality is more than how a person behaves in interaction with others. It is shaped by *how* those other people react and respond. It depends on whether a person is more often rewarded for or deterred from being a certain kind of person. It depends on what kind of personality and what kind of behaviour is rewarded or discouraged, by whom it is rewarded and by whom it is discouraged and the relationship a child has with those people.

Indeed, many things influence a Leaving Cert. student's confidence and feelings of being accepted by others, including some of those listed below:

- The child's physical attractiveness and the way people responded to that.
- The initial temperament of the child, whether this evoked positive or negative responses in others and how these were expressed.
- Demonstrated talents, skills, abilities and whether these were consistent or dissonant with family aspirations. The 'swot' in the sports orientated household is one example. How being different or similar to other family members was received.
- General mood and happiness levels.
- Tendency to be shy or outgoing, dependent or independent, anxious or daring, compliant or challenging, submissive or dominant.
- Sense of humour and capacity to laugh at self, at others, at setbacks and to be amused by situations.
- Whether intense or light-hearted, easy-going or tense, meticulous or careless.
- Optimistic or pessimistic outlook.

Social and Cultural Issues

Ireland has had the good fortune to become, or be on its way to being, truly multicultural. This means greater inclusion of certain groups, such as the Travelling Community, who have their own unique cultural style. It also means identifying as Irish, Irish citizens regardless of racial origins.

Additionally, there are an increasing number of Leaving Cert. students who may not have come through the Irish educational system. They may have had previous positive or negative life experiences depending on the circumstance of their decision to live in Ireland. The following therefore warrant consideration:

- Length of time in the Irish educational system.
- Any circumstance that could have created a sense of difference in the child at any developmental stage, such as being of a different race, being an immigrant or a refugee.
- Experiences of prejudice, discrimination or blatant racism.
- Being the child of a 'foreign adoption' if that is visibly apparent as a racial difference between adoptive parents and child.
- Language proficiency, bilingual experiences and having to switch language in different situations.
- Accent, intonation, tonal quality, language nuances and cultural acceptance or rejection.
- Dress code that is similar or different to that of the majority, and the meaning and interpretation of this by other people.
- Social codes, whether invitations were extended or returned to peers and reciprocated by peers.
- Reactions to differences in behaviour and customs.
- Being a 'foreign' student cut off from family for the duration of second level studies.

Other socio-cultural issues that are significant are the ways that adolescence is discussed in society. This includes the following:

- The way that adolescence as a life stage is discussed in the media and whether this has influenced adults' views and ideas about adolescents or adolescents' views of themselves.
- Other media generated influences and their part in the person's construction of the world.
- Specific educational media reports and programmes. Whether or not they are helpful or create concern in the student's mind.
- The way the Leaving Cert. is talked about and how a person is viewed if they do 'well' or 'badly' in the exam.
- The degree to which the topic is covered on the radio, on TV and in newspaper reports and publications.

Social Skills

Being able to get along with people, feeling confident about meeting new people and having friends is very important. Comrades in adversity are particularly important when a student is doing an exam. When friends are going through the worry and stress of exams, and the other life-stage issues of the Leaving Cert., students do not feel so alone. Factors to consider are the following:

- Capacity to make friends and to keep them.
- The actual number of good friends.
- Relationships with friends, whether life experiences so far have been of acceptance or rejection by others, of being popular or isolated, secure or bullied, anxious or confident, influenced or assertive.
- Sense of comfort with and competence about social rules at each age stage. Knowing how to behave in different settings.
- Socially outgoing or temperamentally shy and the experience of this disposition throughout childhood and adolescence so far.
- Sexual identity and whether or not the person is at ease with men and women of their own age. Whether or not they have a view of themselves as sexual beings and how they interpret

that. Also how that is interpreted for them in society and in the media.

- Level of comfort or concern about that identity
- Finally, having a condition, such as Asperger's Syndrome that make social interactions especially difficult in the teenage years. This deserves special brief discussion because its influence is so extensive in the life of the young person.

Asperger's Syndrome [2]

Asperger's Syndrome must be mentioned specifically under social skills because it is the condition that represents the antithesis of social skill. It is diagnosed and characterised precisely because the person with this condition, despite often good to high intellect, seems to 'get it wrong' when they try to interact with others.

For example Asperger's, which is ten times[3] more frequent in boys than in girls, is typified by difficulties in reading facial expression and social cues, by poor turn-taking in conversation, being very formal, using off putting pedantic ways of talking and by taking meaning literally and often misinterpreting what people are saying. Such young people can't tune in to other people and may bore them about their narrow, repetitive or unusual hobby or interest. They may come too close and not respect personal space, in a way that alienates peers. Being unable to tune in means they are usually left out.

Family Factors

Leaving Cert. students hail from an almost infinite variety of family forms. These are significant in shaping the student. Consider the following:

- Family size and configuration.
- Position in family – eldest, youngest, middle child – and the interpretation of that.

30

- Extended family and the relationships across the generations.
- Family myths, stories, beliefs and the degree to which these have shaped the family ethos.
- Family illnesses, chronic illness in a family member that is a worry.
- Problems of alcoholism in a parent or family member.
- Family violence and the forms that this may have taken.
- Academic, educational status of family members now and in previous generations. Whether or not there are specific career paths the student is expected to take. Whether there is a family business the student is expected to enter into.
- Family talents and the degree to which personal talents have fitted with the talents that are important to other family members.
- Family communication, open, outspoken, upfront or angry, covert, underground.
- Family home, comfort, location and whether or not it is a place that has been open and welcoming to the young person's friends.
- Family style, critical harsh, authoritarian, or warm, supportive and democratic.
- Family separation or divorce. If so, whether this was amicable or hostile. The custody and access arrangements and the management of these.
- Reconstituted family, if parents have remarried whether or not the young person has lived with half siblings, and if this has been in a stable or unstable relationship.
- Warmth and strength of the relationship with other family members, including the extended family.
- Sense of security in the family as a valued family member.

Issues of Self-Esteem

Self-esteem is so central to the well-being of adolescents that it is important to assess the degree to which the Leaving Cert.

student has had good or bad experiences in this regard. The following should be considered:

- The belief the person has in his or her worth and how these beliefs were formed.
- Whether or not the young person currently has high self-esteem or low self-esteem.
- Whether there have been more life experiences of being praised or of being put down.
- The value placed on the young person's opinion and the value the young person places on his or her own view.
- The degree to which the adolescent has felt in control or has felt controlled by other people.
- The level of self-belief and courage to challenge others or the need to follow the crowd.
- The confidence with which tasks in the past have been undertaken.
- How confident the student will be in his or her own ability to cope with the Leaving Cert. year ahead.

Medical and Psychological Factors

Medical and psychological history obviously have huge impact on a child's personal and educational experiences in a way that is complex beyond this chapter's ability to address. However, consider the following:

- Medical conditions and history.
- Accident, injury or serious or critical medical event.
- Chronic illness such as diabetes or asthma. In the case of chronic illness when this was identified, how long it took to identify the illness and how it has been managed since then.
- Minor conditions, which are distressing, particularly at Leaving Cert. stage such as acne, eczema, having to wear glasses or have unsightly braces. Indeed, anything that makes a student feel embarrassed in front of peers.

- Prescribed medications, short-term, long term, effective, side effects and the view of the family and the young person about requiring medication.
- Psychological and psychiatric history, whether there had been any experiences of distress, depression, childhood disorder. If so, how these arose and how they were identified and then managed. Also, the meaning for the family of having someone with such an illness.
- If there have been psychological illnesses, then the student's worries about this. Additionally, the parents worry that the student may not be able to cope with stress, or may become depressed, especially if that has been the experience of the family with another family member.
- Behavioural history, conduct problems, oppositional problems and the current situation.
- Other childhood experiences of psychological import and how they were managed.
- The experience of puberty. The transition into early adolescence and of adolescent life so far.
- Relationship with parents and how that has been perceived and negotiated over the years.

Educational Factors

Age and Educational Experience

While there are some adults who go back to school to access educational opportunities not available in their youth, the majority of Leaving Certificate students are in the older adolescent/young adult stage, aged somewhere between 17 – 19 years. Whether at the lower or upper end of this range depends on the following:

- Age of commencing school, whether early or later.
- Class year repetition or advancement.

- Family difficulties or circumstances affecting school performance.
- Skipping or taking Transition year.
- First time or repeat Leaving Cert. student.

These events will have had their own particular impact on the student. Being the youngest or the oldest in a school year can bring its own pressures, if younger students are trying to keep up with older peers, or older students feel they have outgrown the usual structures and strictures of school life. Educational history also plays its part. The experience of beginning school early or starting school late also often shapes a child's view of study and this will further depend on why the child began school at that age.

Similarly, the circumstances in which a child had to repeat a year at school, whether it was because of illness, learning difficulty, family circumstances, being bullied in a particular class or moving house and school, will have influenced the self-esteem of the student.

Additionally, many students experience Transition Year as a time to acquire new skills and discover hidden potential. It can be an opportunity to test initiative, capacity to self-motivate, to develop maturity and self-confidence and to forge friendships. A student who skips this year may miss out on these developmental advantages.

However, there are some students for whom Transition year does not seem to work well. It can be a time when it distracts them from the momentum of study they had just acquired for the Junior Cert., a momentum they never seem to regain. Unless considerable support is given, there are some students for whom the challenges of demonstrating initiative, imposing self-discipline and engaging in varied social interactions and non-academic activities, diminishes their confidence rather than increases it and leaves them vulnerable when it comes to doing the Leaving Cert.

Other Educational Influences

- Educational achievements to date and the ease or difficulty with which these were achieved. Exam difficulties or successes in the past.
- Relationships with teachers and authority figures.
- The experience of being bullied in school or otherwise ostracised, jeered at, physically threatened or intimidated.
- If the person has behaved as a bully and why they did so.
- Specific disabilities, physical disadvantages, visual and hearing challenges that would influence school adjustment and achievement.
- Whether these were apparent or hidden, embarrassing or acceptable and the degree to which they were experienced as debilitating or otherwise.
- Specific Learning Difficulties, when and how these were identified, and managed.
- Work, vocational or college aspirations.

Finally, there is a world of difference between the student who is going into 6th Year for the first time and the student who is repeating, not to mention the circumstances in which the decision to repeat the Leaving Cert. was taken.

The Leaving Cert. student is, therefore, a person with variations in the following:

- Chronological age,
- Educational experience and opportunity,
- Intellectual and academic skills,
- Social advantage,
- Family circumstances and influences,
- Psychological strength,
- Physical maturity,
- Developmental status.

It helps parents to assess the advantages and disadvantages that their child has experienced and that that young person now brings to this, the Leaving Cert. Year, if they examine the above life experiences.

Certainly there are life experiences that are common to most people growing up and there are other situations that only a few people encounter. Yet each young person setting out to take this exam has accumulated a stunning array of life experiences, which have shaped how he or she will cope in the Leaving Cert. year ahead.

Furthermore there are concerns common to most Leaving Cert. students and these are worth considering at this stage. They are as follows:

Leaving Cert. Students' Fears

The two main life themes that arise for the adolescents at the Leaving Cert. stage are fear and loss. An understanding of the Leaving Cert. student as a person is, therefore, incomplete unless we recognise the fears encountered at this crucial life stage. They are as follows:

- *Fear of failure in the exam.* Also, fear of failing to do what is required in order to get the exam. Many students simply do not know if they can actually organise and structure themselves enough in the year ahead.
- *Fear of success.* Success can heighten expectations about how the young person will achieve in the future. It can cause a gap to open up between a student and friends. It can push the student into making a points-directed choice of third level course instead of one arising from personal interests or talents. It can mean that parents will expect even greater achievements in the future.
- *Fear of disappointing parents.* Many adolescents are primarily concerned with not letting their parents down. Clinical research shows how important it is for young people to make their parents happy and proud of them. The self-esteem of adolescents is closely tied to the esteem in which their parents hold them. If the message to the young person is

that parents are disappointed then it is also a message of acute failure.

- *Fear of 'cracking up'.* The number of reports of adolescents committing suicide generates some of this fear. This makes some young people fearful that they too might succumb to this bewildering and overpowering emotion. After all, if you are a young male who is experiencing exam stress and you are also in the 'at risk' age and stage this is understandable. However, it is important to understand that there are a multitude of factors that would cause a young person to end their life. The Leaving Cert. is rarely if ever the exclusive reason although it may, mistakenly be blamed in these sad circumstances.
- *Fear of not living up to societal expectations.* As discussed in the first chapter of this book, there is so much focus on the Leaving Cert. that it is easy to lose perspective and forget that this is just an exam. The future does not depend on it unless students lose all confidence in themselves because of it.
- *Fear of adulthood.* At this life stage the expectations are that a young person will begin to make adult choices and assume adult responsibilities. The adolescent over eighteen years is legally responsible for him or her self. Adopting adult roles, entering male-female relationships, making career choices, earning personal money, are all part of this stage. That can be overwhelming for some people who do not feel ready to be entirely 'grown-up'.
- *Fear of Change.* Life will never be the same again. The predictability and security of being a school-boy or a school-girl cocooned in childhood is over. Change is always stressful and some changes are more stressful than others. When there is an accumulation of changes co-occurring it is not surprising that Leaving Cert. students become anxious about change.
- *Fear for the future.* Some opportunities will be determined by the results in the Leaving Cert. Choices of apprenticeships, of jobs, choices of third-level courses, college places, many are linked to results in the exam. Worries about failure in the exam get tied to worries about failure in life.

Leaving Cert. Students' Losses

The theme of loss is also very powerful at this life stage and influences how the young person copes during the Leaving Cert. year.

- *Loss of childhood.* Childhood really ends when a person leaves school. Moving from the security of school to the anticipated insecurity of the adult world is a loss that adolescents have to adapt to. Even those who hated school and who can't wait to be out in the world, still experience leaving school as the official departure from childhood.
- *Loss of a way of life.* Again, despite how much young people may hate the school uniform, the regime of the school day, the routine of school and homework and the accountability to adults and to authority, there is also security in these activities that are lost when school is over. The loss is of this predictable way of life.
- *Loss of friends.* Leaving School is one of the first major partings in the life cycle. A child may have begun school at the age of four with people who have remained their friends throughout their school life. The end of school is the first major scattering of friends and for some it is the first lesson in loss. Graduation ceremonies, 'debs' balls and other such rituals heighten this experience for students, and indeed for their parents. There can be a great deal of emotional letting go at the end of the 6th year.
- *Loss of childhood relationship with parents.* Up to this time most young people have been in the role of their parents 'child'. This changes when the young person leaves school. While adolescents often insist that they are grown up from the age of about thirteen onwards, they are nonetheless alarmed when their parents agree. This change of status in parents' eyes usually occurs when the young person leaves school, altering the relationship with parents forever in imperceptible ways. Those who are not ready for independence may resent it being thrust upon them by their parents.

- *Other losses.* Unresolved loss and grief for earlier times often surfaces unexpectedly at this stage. Young people who have suffered *any* previous loss in their life often find the losses of this transition stage particularly painful. If there has been separation or divorce, then the Leaving Cert. year, which is also the final year of childhood, forces the adolescent to accept that the childhood wish for parental reunion will now never occur. Boys and girls whose fathers did not live in the family home can grieve for the fact that they will never have that childhood experience of a father at home.
- *Loss of a parent.* Those young people who have suffered the death of a parent also often encounter particular and unexpected grief at this stage. There can be a wish not to let the dead parent down by doing badly in the exam. There can be sadness that the dead parent will not be around to witness the young person's success. There can be a realisation of the extent of the loss.

Finally, young people can often feel isolated and alone in their individual misery. It can be difficult for them to recognise and articulate all they *are* going through precisely because they are going through it. They may feel deeply anxious and distressed, but be unable to name their fears. Or they may think that all their fears are related to the exam. They may not know how to vent and express their worries or they may do so in inappropriate, unhelpful or even harmful ways that only undermine them further.

Summary

The Leaving Cert. student is not a category, but a specific young person going through an exceptional, transitional life stage. Capacity to cope will depend on all previous life experiences as outlined in this chapter.

It is important that their many fears and feelings of loss associated with this stage of life are understood, normalised, accepted and supported. They must not be left without our respect and help.

We need to remember that the Leaving Cert. student is doing many more kinds of 'Leaving' than the Leaving Cert. exam.

Notes

1 See references and useful reading at back of book.
2 Ehlers, S., & Gillberg, C. (1993) 'The Epidemiology of Asperger Syndrome: A total population study'. *Journal of Child Psychology and Psychiatry* 34, 1327-1350.
3 Gillberg, C. (1995) *Clinical Child Neuropsychiatry,* Cambridge University Press.

3 THE LAST SUMMER

Most parents know that it is important for young people to have a relaxing summer prior to the Leaving Cert. This can go decidedly wrong, however, if the subject of the Leaving Cert. is raised too often. Particularly if it carries the threat of tough times to come, as in the timeworn *'enjoy this while you can because there will be no breaks once you go back to school'*.

That said, the summer months can be put to excellent and advantageous use for the Leaving Cert. student, provided it is with the willing enthusiasm of the student. Parental coercion carries no advantages during the summer months and can set a negative pattern in parent/student communications that ruins the summer for everyone.

There are many students, of course, who like to study in the summer after 5th year, who welcome the opportunity to go into 6th year confident in the knowledge that they've made inroads into a particular subject or subjects.

How the summer is spent, therefore, depends on the individual student.

Some students use the summer prior to 6th year to take formal courses or grinds to provide them with an advantage for the Leaving Cert. year ahead. Students who have set their sights on exceptionally high points, perhaps to acquire entry to a competitive third-level course, may decide that they need the summer to assist them in that challenge.

There are students who use the summer to prepare art portfolios, students who practice for future ballet, dance or drama training courses and students who increase their musical proficiency. There are students who work in hospitals for later careers in nursing, those who work in areas in which they later hope to take a PLC[1] course, or students who get experience in the trade in which they hope to take an apprenticeship after school. Then there are, of course, many students who work for money to ease their financial and social way through the school year ahead.

Some students may benefit from the combination of holiday and learning provided by summer courses or exchanges in countries such as France, Italy, Germany or Spain. Nothing guarantees the improved mastery of language more than a stint in the country in which it is spoken.

Irish College, which offers social, emotional and cultural benefits in addition to language immersion, is usually the first experience many have of this kind of learning.

The foreign language immersion courses set up here in recent years provide an alternative for those who cannot, or do not wish to, travel abroad. Some of these courses are residential; others provide daily programmes, allowing students to enjoy their ordinary social life and evenings free of all thoughts of study.

Then too, there are the subject courses or grinds, which if taken during the summer can dispel fears about a specific subject. This may give a student a feeling of control over a subject that previously was a worry.

But there are many students who say that they simply need a complete summer break to energise them for the task ahead when they go back to school in 6th Year. This is a valid view and a valid request. Some people simply need total distance and disengagement from all things academic to recoup their energies and prepare for the physical and mental requirements of a year of intense study ahead.

If, in the past, the student has shown the capacity to study during the school year and to enjoy the summer months, then it is best to allow this student to continue that successful pattern.

So with the individual needs of the student in mind, the summer should be planned in advance and worked out in an amicable fashion between parents and their children. This can have the added advantage of setting the tone of parent/child discussions about the Leaving Cert. for the next year.

Points for Parents

In their enthusiasm to help their children in their Leaving Cert., many parents fall into the trap of alienating them before the Leaving Cert. year has even begun. There would appear to be a pattern to the kind of conflictual conversations that can take place.

The following have been identified by young people as *the worst kinds* of communication that their parents can make to them during the summer:

- *'You can't lie in bed all day when you go back to school.'*
  Many students protest that they know that. That, they say, is precisely why they are taking the advantage of a lie-in during the holidays. It is important to allow the student to enjoy the summer before the months ahead.

  Students who have a good record of getting up early in the morning and arriving to school on time take justifiable umbrage at the prediction that they will lie in bed all day. They say that they feel aggrieved that their punctuality has not been noted and commended.
- *'I hope you won't be late for school the way you are for your job.'*
  Students who are working in summer jobs also often say that their parents use their summer work performance as a yardstick for their academic commitment. They protest that they are separate commitments undertaken for entirely different motives and often with a different set of skills required.

  Students also say that parents seem to identify the one day that they are late for work to use against them. Summer work is not schoolwork, they argue.

- *'You won't have time to watch that rubbish on TV next year.'*
Summer time, say young people, is a time to watch a bit of trash, relax and chill out. They say that they resent the inference that they will spend the school year in the same way. They say that they want to watch rubbish because next year they will have to focus seriously on subjects and the 'rubbish' is for light summer entertainment. Many also resent the inference that what is of interest to *them* is rubbish.

    Students also often say that if that is their parents' attitude now, in the summer months, by the time the school term arrives they will not get to watch any programme for light relief and necessary relaxation after study. This, they say, increases their anxiety about the year ahead, because it is a year being described as if any type of enjoyment is a criminal activity and that they will, therefore, be imprisoned in the Leaving Cert. school year.

- *'If you are as lazy at school as you are at home, then you'll certainly fail the Leaving.'*
Most young people tend not to prioritise neat bedrooms, clean clothes and washing the dishes every time they use them. They say that having their housework commitment compared with their study commitment is a false argument. They view themselves as being of an age when they have the right to decide about their immediate environment. They see no link whatsoever between the sloppiness of their bedroom and the sloppiness of their academic endeavours.

- *'There'll be no more drinking or going out when you're back at school.'*
There is no doubt that many young people's alcohol use and abuse is a serious issue and one of growing concern. It is important that those who are underage to drink alcohol do not receive a message that drinking is okay. The excessive use of alcohol is also a valid reason for parental worry. However, the two issues of alcohol and study need to be separated to the extent that if the young person is drinking illegally that is one issue, and if they are drinking to excess that is a

further issue. Neither of these circumstances is acceptable, but an argument that links them with study may be perceived as illogical by a young person who sees their time spent drinking alcohol as totally separate from their study time.

If the above statement is made to an eighteen year old who is socialising normally, including having a drink, then it can be perceived as unfair. Such a young person protests that, as for anyone else who works hard and is of a legal age to drink, the entitlement to do so in moderation should not be removed.

The issue of alcohol is one that goes way beyond the issue of study and requires very careful consideration by parents before anything is said about it, either itself or in the context of study.

- *'Would you not do a bit of study now so next year will be easier?'* This statement is usually followed by the suggestion that at the very least some of the plays or poems or history chapters that are time consuming might be read or that maths and science formulae be committed to memory. Students often react to that particular suggestion angrily. This is partly because it is anxiety-provoking. Opening the books feels like beginning the Leaving Cert. process. Additionally, secondary school is still primarily about teacher-guided learning, so that many students simply would not know where to begin.

It is important to remember that the experience of opening the books in summer and then being uncertain of how to study them without the introduction from a teacher or the structure of a homework question can be counterproductive. Only if a student is capable of self-directed study and motivated to do so in summer will it be successful.

- *'You should try doing some of the past Leaving Cert. papers this summer. It's great practise.'* Again students often feel that because they have not yet finished the subject course, that there is no logic whatsoever in attempting the final paper in that subject. There is nothing more likely to raise anxiety levels than to sit a paper on a course in which you have only had partial familiarity or teaching. At the end of 5th year only a certain portion of many courses has been covered.

However, if some work on the exam papers is to be done during the summer, what some students find useful is to select a few topics or questions that have already been covered in class and set about constructing an answer to those questions. Going into 6th year with a number of 'model' type answers already prepared, in the event of certain topics arising in the exams, is very helpful and reassuring.

In summary, regardless of the fine intent of parents, the above statements/suggestions seem to be the ones that lead to most parent/student conflict during the summer prior to 6thYear.

Parents Points

Obviously, in any debate or negotiation, it is useful to hear both sides of the argument. While many a well-intentioned parental statement can be anxiety-provoking, contentious or illogical to their pre-Leaving Cert. offspring, there are also many sound reasons for parents to make some of the above suggestions. The rationale behind many, and the reason parents make such seemingly offensive comments in the first place, may not be immediately apparent to the student.

The following are the points that parents often make in response to being castigated by their children for suggesting that the summer be productively used in the interest of the Leaving Cert. exam:

• They worry about their children lying in bed all day. They are afraid that a sleep/wake pattern of staying up very late and lying in bed during the day developed in the summer will be hard to break on the return to school.
• Parents often know how long it takes their own children to adjust their schedules and that unless they have some

routine, at least in late summer, the adjustment will be too precipitous and difficult when September arrives. This is why the parent who watches their child rise at lunchtime, having watched videos into the early hours of the morning, feels compelled to issue the reminder that a new schedule will be in place in autumn.

- Watching a young person deadlining and being late for a job, naturally makes parents worry that that spirit of timekeeping will continue into 6th year and disadvantage their child.
- Equally, watching their offspring mentally vegetate as they sit in front of the TV screen worries them that an addiction will be formed that will be hard to break when school begins.
- Parents say that they tend to interpret the commitment given to one task as an example of the capacity of the person to commit to another task. Signs of laziness are, therefore, worrying in case the same slovenliness will come into schoolwork in the Leaving Cert.
- Alcohol is a serious worry to parents, who are concerned about increasing evidence of the problem of alcohol in the lives of young people. Even when a young person is legally of an age to drink, parents are aware of the addictive nature of alcohol and know that the habits of drinking formed during the summer might not be broken as easily as the young person thinks they will be. Issuing warnings is one way of indicating this concern and reminding the young person that alcohol, if taken at all, must be used wisely in the school year ahead.
- Some parents *do* believe that even a little study during the summer would ease pressure when the student is back at school. They say that they suggest this based on the knowledge of their own child. For example, if their child has had a problem with a particular subject in 5th year or if they have noted that their child becomes overwhelmed when too much revision has to be done in a short time.
- Similarly, the suggestion of tackling exam papers is based on a parent's knowledge that familiarity with exam papers is

often reassuring and also helps to guide a student's learning to relevant aspects of the course. They say that they do not expect the child to be able to formally sit the entire paper. It is just an opportunity to gain acquaintance with format and content.

Benefits of Summer Study

There is no doubt that the summer prior to 6th Year can be a most profitable preparatory time for many students about to enter the Leaving Cert. year in a whole variety of ways.

Psychological Benefits

- It can provide an opportunity to catch up.
- Summer grinds can give confidence to a student who has a difficulty with a particular subject.
- Worry may be diminished or removed. The anticipation of an event is often worse than the event itself. Getting down to some study during the summer months means that worry about the year ahead does not fester and grow.
- Subjects that are particularly extensive or time-consuming can overwhelm students during the short academic year. This tendency to panic may be offset by familiarity with extensive subjects during summer. Students who are prepared are less likely to feel overwhelmed at a later stage.
- Looking through exam papers to gain familiarity with the type and style of questions can be reassuring. This can also attune a student to the kind of information that is often required in examinations thereby assisting a more focused, question-related way of studying on return to school.
- Courses on stress management may be undertaken so that the student has a set of skills to alleviate stress on entering 6th year. For example, some students take up yoga, 'autogenic' training, transcendental meditation or join fitness clubs to help them control feelings of anxiety that may arise in the months ahead.

- Training in biofeedback,[2] which provides a way of controlling involuntary physical or physiological feelings of panic, can be engaged in. This is particularly useful for those students who tend to have panicky feelings that they feel they cannot control.
- The role of natural perfumes and odours in mood alteration is increasingly understood. Provided there are no medical contraindications, this is the time to try out herbs, plants and oils that increase concentration, assist memory or protect immunity.

Learning and Memory Skills

- Summer time can be an opportunity to learn the tricks of learning. Strategies and tips for learning can be examined so that students may enter 6th year with an armoury of good study devices.
- Memory skills may be developed. This is often an opportunity to learn about mnemonics, acronyms, memory rhymes, using mental imagery, visualisation, and other short and long-term memory strategies. Summer provides the opportunity to play board games that require memory. Many simple card games such as 'pick a pair' help to train memory.
- Students who need to 'overlearn' or revise continuously in order to remember can commit specific material to memory during the non-stressful summer months. Unless we undertake deliberate repetition and rehearsal of certain kinds of information, particularly factual information, we forget it. Obviously the higher the number of times we expose ourselves to a story, a book, a poem, a fact, a formula, a graph, a map, the greater our likelihood of recall. This is a good time to learn cell mitosis, basic genetics and photosynthesis, which regularly appear on exam papers.
- Specific information, such as dates of battles, lists of places, names of characters, benefit by being learned during a non-stressful time and in a creative way as this improves the initial intake of this information, its storage and retrieval.

- Specific techniques, which are time consuming initially to learn, but which, having been acquired, allow the efficient organisation of large quantities of information, such as Buzan's[3] mind-mapping techniques can be studied.

Computer skills

- The ideal time to learn and practise typing skills and word-processing skills is summer. Acquiring these skills allows the student to do tasks that usually involve writing much more rapidly. On return to school they can, therefore, take notes from books, do the first draft of homework assignments and make summary notes.
- Later in the year important revision notes can be prepared more quickly by word-processor. Additionally, having typed notes means that students can retain their study notes and essays in a neat, compact and accessible way.
- Summer can also be a time to learn how to structure ideas in written form. Again, word-processing is ideal and many students now construct their essays using a word-processor, make the changes, use the spell-check and then transcribe a well-thought out, edited, correctly-spelt, finished product to hand in to school.
- Of course, there are some students who are granted what is called 'special consideration' in the exam because of dyslexic problems. These can include problems in writing at speed and in some instances they have been allowed to type their exam answers. Obviously, for such students familiarity with the computer and speed of typing is important.
- In summary, proficiency using the computer for practical day-to-day activities is important for every student in this technological age and should be acquired before going back to school. Summer is a good time to acquire speed and efficiency in word-processing.

Practical Planning

- Some students use summer to undertake a range of peripheral activities so that they will not have to be undertaken during the academic year. For example, this is a good time to have general health and fitness checks, to get any necessary dental work done, to plan orthodontic appointments.
- Having acne is upsetting and stressful for young people. If persistent acne has been a problem for them, then summer is a good time to have this investigated so that remedies and treatment options might be tried. Appearance and confidence are intensely connected at the Leaving Cert. stage of life.
- If a student has their own mode of transport – bike, motorbike or car – this is the time to have them serviced and in good working order for the school year. Advance preparation of everything assists a smoother year ahead.
- This is also the time to organise one's bedroom and clear out all the unnecessary junk that might have accumulated over the winter months. The less cluttered the space the more a student feels in control of it.
- If, as noted earlier, a student has decided to enjoy the assistance of aromatherapy, then summer is a good time to have an aromatherapy consultation. Clearly, experimentation with oils should not be left to 6th Year, just in case there are any contraindications or reactions. For example, rosemary oil, can be burnt, inhaled, sprinkled or misted in a study setting. This has particularly been identified as being beneficial to learning and memory, but equally there are some instances where individuals are advised against use of specific oils or oil combinations. It is better to know what suits the individual student before the school year begins.
- Some students like to learn about colour therapy and, perhaps, take the opportunity to paint their bedroom or place of study. Colour therapists say that yellow is

particularly identified as the colour most likely to promote study because it is supposed to stimulate the logical, left side of the brain. Green is considered to be a calm, soothing colour that is suitable for anyone who is troubled, while red has always been associated with power and energy and, of course, with challenge. However too much can be too challenging.

- At the end of the day each teenager must choose the colour with which they feel most comfortable, most alert, energised and also most restored. In other words, the colour most conducive to their study. There are advantages and disadvantages to all colours and colour combinations. When each student has chosen their own environment, it is good to spend time during the summer in the room that you hope will be study-conducive in the year ahead, just to test if the colour works as intended.

Academic Benefits

- As already noted, summer can provide time for immersion in a language bringing fluency to a much higher level. Allied to this students who gain some oral fluency also often find that the prescribed texts in that language can become more comprehensible.
- In practical areas such as art, technical drawing, mechanical drawing and woodwork, creativity can be fostered, designs can be experimented with and practical skills can be refined
- In Home Economics, recipes can be tried out. This is an enormous aid to memory at a later stage when there is so much to remember in this extensive subject.
- Museums can be visited to assist art appreciation for the student of Art. What has been viewed in a gallery is much more likely to be remembered than what has been read about our looked at in a book.
- Concerts can be attended by those taking Music as a Leaving Certificate subject. It goes without saying that the true

musician will be maintaining practise and play on their chosen musical instrument during the summer.

- The theatre can be attended, particularly if a prescribed Leaving Cert. play is being staged. This brings a lively reality to what otherwise can seem to be irrelevant dry texts. But even if course content is not actually being staged, many parents take the opportunity to enjoy the light summer theatre programmes with their children, which increases their sense of connection to this art form.
- Videos or DVDs of prescribed texts in English Literature, in Irish studies, in Classical Studies or Greek and Roman Mythology can be viewed.
- Courses in writing skills or editing can be taken, providing a practical skill for essay writing and the preparation of assignments in addition to a life-long improvement in written self-expression.
- Audiotapes of poems will bring familiarity to material.
- Schedules of study for the year ahead may be planned during the summer.
- Finally, it is good to set aside time in the summer for preparation of a place to study and acquisition of all the practical materials such as pens, pencils, refill pads that are likely to be needed for the year ahead. This ensures that as much as possible is organised before actually returning to school.

The Leaving Cert. year will end. By the end of the year summer will have returned. Whatever was to be achieved will have been achieved.

The battles, fears, hopes, anxieties and worries will be over and parents and young people will look back on the Leaving Cert. Year, surprised that so much could be over in such a short time.

The year and the exam will be seen in perspective and parents and young people will move on to the next battle, what might be called the 'Ibiza Syndrome'.[4] This is the big battle between parents and children about whether the Leaving Cert.

'celebratees' are safe abroad kicking up their heels after a hard year of study.

But that is next year, the end of this book. That is the time of rest and relaxation and reprieve before the next summer battle and the next academic onslaught of adjustment to Third Level.

In the meantime, as parents would say to their children, there is work to be done.

Notes
1   PLC. The Post-Leaving Certificate which began in 1985. There are more than 240 colleges offering PLCs. Students are now entitled to a third-level maintenance grant if eligible.
2   Carrol, D. (1984) *Biofeedback in Practice*, Longman, New York.
3   Buzan, T. (2001) *Headstrong: How To Get Physically and Mentally Fit*, Thorsons, London.
4   See Chapter 15, 'The Ibiza Syndrome'.

4

GETTING STARTED

Summer is over. The schools have re-opened. Sixth year has begun. This is the first day back to school in 6th year and the last day back to school in the adolescent's life. It is an emotional time for both parents and children.

First Day of 6th Year

Young people describe many emotions on this first day. These range from delight to be on the final lap of school to terror at the year ahead.

For parents, too, the first day of the last year at school is significant in a way that is hard to articulate, but probably understood by all parents. Perhaps it is because it is a marker, the last year of childhood, the culmination of school life, a competitive test ahead in which their child may succeed or fail.

To add to the strangeness of these unvoiced feelings, after all, the child has been *going back to school* for close on twelve years already, is the contradictory familiarity of the event. On the one hand this seems like a repetition of every other first day back at school. On the other hand, parents feel that they are facing into unknown territory if they haven't parented a Leaving Cert. student before.

Anxiety has to find a focus and a great deal of anxiety gets concentrated on this first day. So much so that the pattern of student/parent communication that may predominate *during* the year, if it has not been determined during the summer, often gets laid down on this day.

Other factors may also colour that first day back, not least of which is the way the summer was spent, particularly if either parent or child harbour resentments about the discussions that have already taken place during the summer about the Leaving Cert. It is important that parents do not begin warnings on the first day back at school – it frightens the already worried, angers the motivated and de-motivates the student who has already decided to surprise parents with their studiousness. Some may even scrap their good intentions if they are commanded to study. Students often refer to the following:

- The number of times over the summer the student was warned about 6th year.
- The anxiety created when the Leaving Cert. results came out in August, particularly if there were remarkable achievements by the offspring of friends and relations, now on the road to success in their chosen courses.
- Allied to this, aspirations set on the basis of these other peoples' results, or career possibilities that are of no interest to the student.
- Equally daunting, hearing the results of the offspring of friends and relations' children who did *not* get the points they desired or the places they aspired to.
- Pessimistic predictions about the end of all opportunity after a poor Leaving Cert., with the implication that *'if X couldn't manage it, what hope have you'*.
- This lack of faith in the student to manage the year ahead is upsetting. Worse still is the burden of too much faith in the student to cope with everything.
- Knowing that there will be teacher 'pep talks' in each class on return to school and the expectation on arrival home that the short day at school will have generated hours of homework.
- Not being able to 'ease back' into school with a little mental warm-up before strenuous exertion. Instead, having to study

the first day back, just to reassure parents that this will be the pattern to come.
- Finally, inner fear about ability to cope now that the much warned about 'year' has arrived.

Parents in turn have their views of the first day and tend to attribute the strain to the following:

- Inexplicable emotions. The end of an era, last year in school. Feeling of protectiveness towards their child allied to a need to encourage the students' maturity and independence in work and study.
- Fear for the future. Anxiety about their child being unprepared for the competitive world that lies ahead. Acute sense of responsibility as a parent to the student
- Needing some statement from the student at the start of term that the year is significant and will not be wasted. Therefore, wanting everyone to begin as they intend to continue.
- Their own memories of Leaving Cert. and whether it was a happy or difficult time for them.
- If parents did not have the opportunity to study for the Leaving Cert., being angry that their children take for granted or dismiss what would have been a precious opportunity for them.
- If they achieved well in the Leaving Cert., but were denied studying further, finding it hard to understand why a student would not aspire to the opportunities the parent missed out on.
- If parents have made financial sacrifices to provide the student with educational advantage, feeling hurt that this hard work is being negated.
- Recognising, as their child leaves school, that they, as parents, have reached a certain life-cycle stage, which is bringing them into the middle-years of established adulthood. Wondering what it is all about, this cycle of life stages.

- Fears that their child may not be able to do what it takes to succeed in the Leaving Cert. and concern about how the child will cope with failure should it occur. Equally, having questions about how the student may handle success.

Parents' Points

Additionally many parents say that at the beginning of the year, they wish they could communicate the following to their children:

- That they are genuinely trying to be helpful to their children and do not always know how to achieve that.
- That they are afraid to push them and afraid not to push them. They are afraid of the consequences for their children of both approaches.
- That it upsets them if well-intentioned inquiries get misconstrued as criticism. They point out that *asking is not accusing* and that many of the questions that they ask their children are attempts to show their interest and concern.
- Similarly, if they ask questions about study that those questions are an attempt to understand how the student feels so that they can help if necessary.
- That they do *not* expect their children to succeed beyond their capacity to do so. They say that they simply want them to do as well as they can.
- That they may find it difficult to maintain a balance between providing support and taking what is, at the end of the day, the student's responsibility. That is a difficult balance to maintain at the beginning of 6th year when they want their student to begin well and form good study habits.
- That their motives are not self-aggrandisement. They want their children to do well in the Leaving Cert. so that it will open up options for them in the future.
- That they will measure success by the *effort* the student puts into study rather than exam achievement.

- That they love their children regardless of their capacity to succeed academically. However, they are aware that more arguments often erupt with the child who won't study because they feel an obligation to protect that child from the later consequences of this.
- That they don't always know how to tell their children they love them.
- Finally, on this first day on the brink of this Leaving Cert. year, the exam is not more important than their children's health and happiness.

How to Get Started

Research shows us that it is the quality of study we do rather than just the quantity that is most important.

The start of the year is the time for students, with the help of their parents, to wipe the slate clean on the past and prepare for the months ahead. If students have not managed to get organised before 6th year, then this is the time for them to be focused, time-managed, structured and even strategic.

This begins with setting out a place to study, then knowing *when* to study, *what* to study, *how* to learn and *what* kind of attitude is needed to succeed. These are the first tasks to be considered on the first day of 6th year.

Where to Study

It may seem obvious, but having a specific place in which to study is important. Research suggests that we need to condition ourselves to study in the same place, if possible at the same time and in the same way to make the most of our time. In other words, to set up a pattern of study that makes study a regular and predictable habit rather than a chore to be got through each day.

This is not to say that any one pattern is superior to another, but having a routine is crucial and students need to learn what routine suits them best.

Places to Study
- All students benefit by having a place that is comfortable and conducive to study. If possible, it should be bright and cheerful, have good lighting, be away from too much noise and have adequate heat and ventilation.
- The settling in time to study is reduced if it takes place in the same location. The place becomes associated with study, which helps concentration.
- If it is too warm and too cosy then it will induce sleep not study. If it is arctic it will freeze the brain as well as the body.
- A clock near the desk, preferably one with an alarm, is useful. Some students set the alarm for hourly study sessions and decide not to leave the study area until the alarm goes off.
- The traditional idea of a clear space or desk with plenty of room for notes, a set of shelves for easy access to books and files, an upright chair, and peace and quiet still holds true.
- If parents can provide a desk and shelves, that helps to get the student organised. These have become very inexpensive and some desks contain a filing drawer and small drawers for pens and pencils, highlighters, erasers and staplers and all the accoutrements of study.
- Some parents invest in an orthopaedic back chair for their students. These are essentially chairs on which one kneels, very comfortable, and they ensure great posture by preventing curving the back, slumping shoulders or leaning over the desk. Alternatively, a good supportive chair will help.
- An adjustable desk-lamp ensures that light falls on the page and reduces eyestrain. The light should be turned on when the student begins to study, otherwise students sometimes do not notice that darkness is descending and can study in poor lighting conditions unawares.

Study Aids
- A good dictionary and thesaurus are important. There are also pocket versions of these, which are small, light and can be carried around. It is suggested that a student might consider flicking through the dictionary during spare

moments, for example, waiting for a bus. This is an excellent way to extend vocabulary.

- Also an alphabetically sectioned notebook into which vocabulary and phrases and ideas that are useful for essays may be written. This is convenient, also, for keeping those words that the student tends to misspell. It is interesting that people tend to continuously misspell a small number of words. Making a personal list of those and checking spelling each time can alter this.

Notice Board

- A large notice board should be fixed to the wall above the desk on to which information can be pinned. This space should be used. For example, it should contain important maths formulae, the period table of elements, quotations – perhaps from the prescribed Shakespearian play for the Leaving – to be memorised, an entire poem that is on the course, the school timetable with the time and location of activities for each day clearly marked.
- Reminders for PE gear and sports activities should be highlighted. A timetable of the dates on which homework assignments are due should be displayed prominently.
- At the beginning of each study session the study plan for the next hour should also be pinned on this board in the eye-line of the student so that when the student looks up the plan helps to refocus.
- There are specific laminated cards, which can be bought, that contain verbs and grammar in a number of languages. There are some that contain frequently misspellt words in English. These can also be displayed nearby. Whatever the use, having a board, is like an external mental reminder, a great stress reducer and an important part of the study environment.

Colour-Coding

- All subjects should be colour coded. This means that a different colour is assigned to each subject. For example students might choose red for Maths, green for Irish, blue for French, purple for Science, depending on what the students initial connection is between the subject and a colour.

- Organise *all* notes into folders coloured to match each subject. Make sure that the colours chosen are also the colours that will be used to draw margins, put in headings and identify the copybook or the refill sheet every time a subject is studied.
- Students should also have some boxes, allocated to the different subjects, each box in the colour allocated to that subject. Free or cheap cardboard boxes can be used or large plastic boxes can be bought.

Boxes and Filing

- Into these boxes newspaper cuttings and articles of relevance to the subject can be collated, notes can be placed in them until there is an opportunity to file them appropriately. In other words, the boxes ensure that the students' notes are never untidy, muddled with other subjects, crumpled or lost.
- Additionally, if parents find students' books lying around the house they can be returned to the boxes dedicated to those subjects
- At the end of each school day, students can organise the contents of their school bags into the relevant boxes before beginning the night's study. This is really a filing system for the brain.

Technological Aids and Distractions

- If the student is lucky enough to have a computer, this needs to be restricted to use for study or located elsewhere in the house. Otherwise the study environment will become a relaxation one and confuse the study pattern. Computer games can be highly addictive. It does not make sense to have the temptation of the computer in the study area.
- It is also preferable that the study area does not contain a TV or CD player. This is because the retrieval during an exam of

what has been learnt when listening to music is reportedly *less than* what has been learnt in silence. Having said that, there are some reports that listening to Mozart is mentally conducive to learning and concentration.

- Furthermore, there are some 'concentration' tapes and CDs available, which emit sounds that are said to stimulate brain activity and enhance learning. If music is to be played, however, it is advised that it be without distracting lyrics or dissonant sounds. If Mozart works he should play on. However, neither the students' CDs nor Mozart will be available on the day of the exam, so reliance on either may be ill-advised.

Finally, wherever the student studies, whatever type of space it is, whether music is played or not, what is important is that the student chooses the best possible study place, as it can have an ongoing influence on how they experience 6th year.

When to Study

It is important to know what a student's best study times are, and for what activities. The following are suggested:

- Students should know their peak study times, when energy is highest. This may be early in the morning before school or later in the evening. A time table is not just about spending time, but about allocating tasks to that time.
- Students are advised to tackle the more difficult tasks during these peak energy times. They can keep routine organising, filing, proofing and transcribing for the times of greater fatigue.
- Some students prefer to launch straight into homework on return from school. Others prefer to have a rest and then begin with a review of the class notes for the day, while others find this is a good time to commit material to memory.

- There are students who become drowsy after a meal and find that this is the best time to take a break or a walk.
- There are students who find the refuelling of a meal makes them more alert for difficult tasks.
- Whatever a student's pattern, it is important for each student to keep track of their own peak study times and allocate the different learning tasks according to the mental energy they require.

What to Study

Knowing what to study does not just mean knowing what subjects to study. It means having an actual breakdown of each subject into small, manageable, comprehensible units that can be studied at one sitting. This is one of the first and most important tasks of 6th year. How to achieve this is somewhat detailed but it deserves a full description. The steps provided below are as follows:

1   Students should gather their textbooks from 5th year and any new books they may acquire for 6th year and examine the list of *contents* in each book. This means that the student knows exactly *what* they are meant to know from their textbooks by the end of the year.

2   A list should then be made of each of the chapters in *each* of the books. This is the first step to writing out a study timetable. It is the contents of courses, which will later be divided into study units over the days and weeks ahead.

3   Alternatively, some people prefer to photocopy the front pages of their textbooks, those pages on which the chapters are listed and described. This can be particularly helpful if the front pages also provide a summary of what is contained in each chapter.

4   When all of these lists or photocopied pages have been gathered, the student then has a 6th year contents list.

Some students supplement this with the information that comes from the official curriculum for 6th year.

5 Others make a list by going through each chapter of their books and writing out all the headings and subheadings. This has the added advantage of bringing the student through each page of their books and providing an overall familiarity with the layout, style, tone, chapter sizes, headings and content in each course. Occasionally they may even linger at sections that attract their interest or attention. Now that is true study!

6 Regardless of how a student chooses to collate information on what they need to know, students will realise that one cannot begin to study without knowing *what* is to be studied.

7 If a student has any doubt about what is required in a subject, teachers in school can provide this information and are the best people to ask about this.

8 Study can then be broken down into small, manageable units from each chapter and these can be written into the timetable.

9 The student then begins to do two things. One is to study and the other is to revise. Students should aim to do a mixture of *study* (that is learning new material) and *revision* (that is viewing again, reviewing, anything that was previously taught and studied). This establishes the important early pattern in 6th year of study and revision, important because constant revision is required in order to retain information.

10 Research shows us that without revision we forget most of what we learn. Keeping revision alive *as a set part of each day and each week* is, therefore, imperative.

11 Finally getting down to good study at the beginning of the year, and doing consistent revision, removes the need to cram massively in the final weeks before the Leaving Cert. A steady input of material into the memory system is what commits information to long-term memory. This is much better than the over-crammed short-term memory in

which a student hopes to retain information overnight until it is expunged in an exam the next day.

How to Learn

One of the mistakes that students often make when studying is to make broad decisions such as 'tonight I will study Physics or English'. This is akin to deciding to 'go for a walk' without planning what direction to take, where the walk will begin or end and what will be viewed en route.

- There must always be a planned route when setting out to study. Deciding to work on pages 5-15 of Chapter 2 in History is an entirely different proposition to deciding to 'study History'. One is a definite goal, the other too often a pious aspiration. When a student does not have a plan, then studying becomes an impossible task.
- It is important that the plan includes full attendance at school. It is amazing how much information is taken in simply by being in school consistently. Concepts have a chance to build upon each other, whereas when classes are missed, the rest of the class have often moved on to another idea when the student returns. Much of learning is like building a tower of blocks, miss one part and the structure can fall down.
- Learning includes benefiting from the school day by listening in class, reflecting on what has been heard in class and fitting that into what the student already knows, making notes and jotting down points. Writing notes can help us learn.
- We also learn by explaining something to another person. We remember at least 50 per cent of what we explain to another straight away, and if we cannot explain it then we need to revise it.
- Students can also listen to how people make points on TV or radio programmes. Is what they are saying and *how* they are

saying it clear? Keeping abreast of current affairs is important in 6th year, as it is not uncommon for one of the essay options to be on an issue of public debate. This mental editing or ordering of information is good practise for organising ideas for assignments or debate.

- It is important to begin the preparation of study cards, quick reminders or maps of key points that the student will carry around for ongoing revision.
- People have different methods of learning. For example, some students find that they retain what they *hear*, others that they retain what they *see* and still others that their best means of remembering is by *doing*, or what is called *procedural* learning. It is interesting that research shows that we retain much better what we learn in this procedural way.
- Understanding one's learning style means knowing the different ways in which individual students process information and each student knowing their own particular style. Styles include the following (1) *Concrete*, when one learns best by doing, acting sensing and feeling. (2) *Active* style, where one learns by making use of new information. Students who opt for the Applied Leaving Cert.[2] often have these concrete and active kinds of learning style and creativity. (3) *Abstract* style is learning by observation and analysis (4) *Reflective* style is when the student learns by thinking and reflecting on the experience.
- Each student should find their personal 'best' learning method and then use it. For some students listening to audiotapes will help, for others they remember by retaining a visual image and so videotapes will work best. For still others, planning and mapping out the material in diagrams works best. It is important at this stage that students decide what their own preferred method of learning and remembering is and that they begin to use it *every* time they study.
- The more modes of learning we employ the better we learn, retain and retrieve information. This so-called multi-modal learning is important because it combines the different learning modes of reading, seeing, hearing, saying and

doing. If we combine these methods and revise regularly, our retention of information is raised as high as 90 per cent.

- In addition to modes of learning, students need to attend to their ways of remembering what they have learnt. The stages of memory are intake (encoding), storage and retrieval. There is also short-term memory and long-term memory. Long-term memory is required for exams. Obviously for an exam there is a need to take in information or encode it in a way that allows it to be stored during the Leaving Cert. year and retrieved during the actual exam.

- Students need to understand what they are learning in order to take in the information. It gets stored more effectively if it is organised and accompanied by images that help memory, for example people often remember something because the accompanying picture in their book reminds them of it. Also, it is retrieved better if the student practises retrieving it when learning it. For example, imagine learning the lines of a poem, and after each verse trying to say it aloud. This is retrieval at the time of learning, which commits the verse to memory.

- It is usual to recommend that students use the now famous five stages for learning known as PQRST[3] or *Preview, Question, Read, Self-Recitation and Test*. *Preview* is when a student skims through a chapter or chapters in a book noting how it is organised, the headings, and the layout. *Questions* is obviously asking questions about what has been previewed and *Read* involves answering those questions. *Self-recitation* means trying to remember the main ideas preferably by saying them out loud. Finally *Test* is testing memory of the important facts.

- Students who use this way of studying will find that they are revising as they study, storing as they learn and retrieving as they store. It is a powerful means of learning.

- Other students like to rely on visual maps, diagrams and mind maps and find that the Buzan[4] Mind-Mapping method is most helpful. 'Mind Maps' make notes that use key words and images, so they are quick to make and easy to remember.

They are visual and colourful, compact, and great for learning, creativity and revision.

- If you have not done mind-maps they have some similarity to 'spidergrams', so called because they are diagrams that resemble spiders. The 'body' represents the main subject area and the 'legs' the important points that one would wish to make about that topic.
- To make a spidergram begin with a large circle into which you put the topic heading. For example take the topic of the World Cup. Then extend out several 'legs', each one representing a piece of information; number of teams, criteria for qualification, location of the matches, the social, cultural and national significance, the economic advantages, such as flags sold, memorabilia, team colours. 'Legs' might represent cost to the economy, days off work or money spent travelling to foreign matches. Another 'leg' might list the teams that were eliminated, the sequence of eliminations and the country that won. Finally, the psychological significance, national, moral and attraction of young people to sports.
- Another strategy, already mentioned, that helps learning is colour coding.[5] This creates a filing system in the brain and assists memory by associating a colour with material to be learned.
- Knowing how to study includes knowing when NOT to study. A student should stop if they feel tired or unwell, if they are making too many mistakes or not taking in information, or if they are becoming upset or overly anxious.
- Finally, a point that will be repeated at intervals throughout the book is the importance of recreating examination conditions. That is because this is one of the best methods of learning and retaining information. Each piece should be studied while imagining answering a question on that topic in the exam. There is nothing more likely to focus the mind than pretending that this is the real thing!

The start of 6th year is the start of the 'real thing'.

Student Attitude

Sometimes students do not take time alone to reflect on the meaning of the exam for them. Just for them, personally. The beginning of 6th year is the time for students to ask themselves some of these questions.

It is impossible to succeed if students feel that they are being carried along on a course that is not of their choosing. It is difficult if they are entering this year because they have no option, if it is just something that *has* to be done at the end of secondary school.

Students should ask themselves the following questions:

- *'What are my feelings about this exam?'* They should write them down. They may include words such as fear, pressure, excitement, confidence, challenge, or opportunity.
- *'What are my fears?'* Fear of not remembering anything in the exam, of going blank, of having to repeat, of wasting parents' money, of letting self or parents down, of not succeeding as well as brothers or sisters or cousins, of being found out, of not being as clever as people thought.
- *'What are my expectations of myself?'* Are they realistic? Are they pessimistic or optimistic? Are the goals too high or are they achievable?
- *'Who will be most pleased if I succeed?'* Is it my parents, my friends, my teachers, girlfriend, my boyfriend or myself? It is helpful for students to examine the network of relationships in which they are engaged and how these people connect with the student and the student's exam results. Sometimes a student feels they have to make up for the disappointing results of an older sibling so parents will not be disappointed a second time. Sometimes a student thinks they have to live up to a sibling's excellent results or feel a 'failure' in the family.
- *'Is there anyone who will be disappointed if I achieve?'* Am I in competition with a boyfriend, with peers, with classmates with other family members, brothers or sisters?

- *'Who will be most disappointed if I do not achieve?'* How has that been conveyed by that person to the student? Again students should explore how they feel about this responsibility not to disappoint others. Is it real or imagined? If the person were asked about their possible disappointment would they be surprised the student felt this way? Would they confirm the student's feelings or reassure them?
- *'What do I need to succeed?'* Is it psychological confidence, practical intervention such as classes, grinds, family support, more time, and relief from paid work? The student should identify everything required to achieve. A brain-storm session, writing down everything that pops into the student's head, often reveals some important previously unidentified difficulty or needs.
- *'Who can help me?'* Does the student know at all times how to seek help for whatever arises over the course of the year?
- *'Do I believe that I can succeed with work?'* This is a crucial question because students who deep down do not think they can succeed set themselves on a particularly difficult course.
- *'What would stop me?'* This is the place for the student to list all the obstacles, emotional, academic, family, practical, personal.
- *'Who would stop me?'* Are there peers or relationships – maybe a boyfriend or girlfriend – that would distract from study or make it difficult to study? This can happen if a student's friends are older or have left school or if they are not educationally committed.
- *'What are the subjects I feel confident about?'* These should be listed and detailed.
- *'What subject worries me most?'* If a student is taking that subject at higher level this may be the time to consider whether to change to ordinary level, to discuss the concern with parents or teachers and perhaps set a time limit, such as Christmas, in which a decision will be taken about changing to ordinary level.
- *'Have I too much pressure?'* Is the student taking too many subjects? Should one subject be dropped? If too many

subjects are tipping the balance of pressure on the student how can that be addressed?

- *'How have I coped before under pressure?'* Is the student confident in the capacity to manage stress? Is this reassuring or worrying to the student?
- *'Am I afraid of trying?'* Many students do not realise that they fear studying really hard in case they fail despite all the hard work. This would mean that they might be perceived as being 'stupid'. They think that it would be preferable to be seen as not having tried than be seen as having tried and failed. This is an issue that requires attention at the beginning of 6th year or it can sabotage a student unconsciously.
- *'How can I change my attitude?'* If I continue to hold these views will I succeed or fail? There is considerable support for the idea that deciding one will succeed is part of success. Telling oneself positive things about one's worth enhances self-esteem.
- Finally, some affirmations, such as *I can do this, I am confident, I can study and I can succeed* printed out and posted where the student can see them and repeat them daily are conducive to positive thinking.

Sometimes *saying is believing*. It is worth a try.

Notes

1 This has been described as 'The Mozart Effect' (see refs. Campbell, D.G.). Other studies have shown that listening to Baroque music while studying can enhance one's ability to memorise spellings, poetry and foreign words.
2 The Leaving Cert. Applied is a self-contained two-year programme introduced in 1995 with a cross-curricular approach rather than a subject-based structure. Students complete 40 modules each of 40 hours in addition to task assessments and external examinations
3 See ref. Study by Thomas & Robinson in 1982.
4 Mind mapping technique for learning and memory (see refs. Buzan).
5 See Chapter 4 for description of this.

5

STUDENTS' POINTS FOR PARENTS

Many parents speculate about their children's needs during the Leaving Certificate year. They want to be kind, supportive, respectful, facilitative and encouraging. They want to be realistic about their children's strengths, abilities, academic needs and potential. They do not want to pressurise beyond the student's apparent intellectual capacity or psychological strength.

Equally, they do not want to neglect their parental duty in a way that would affect exam performance negatively or fail to bring out the ability and potential of their particular child.

Pressure or Neglect?

Parents who decide to leave the young person to their own devices often feel guilty that they may be reneging on their parental responsibility. They worry that they will be blamed if their child fails to obtain a good Leaving Cert. or to gain the necessary points for a chosen course or career.

They also believe that if their Leaving Cert. student is too immature to study, then the onus is on them, as parents, to ensure that sufficient study is done. Otherwise, in later years, when the recalcitrant student has become a mature young adult, they, the parents will be blamed. Sentences such as *'why didn't you make me study?'* come to mind and no parent wants to live under the spectre of their child perceiving them as having neglected their educational needs by being too uncaring to get actively involved.

This parental fear is not unfounded. There are parents out there who have been blamed in later years by their children for not recognising that their sons or daughters were too immature and naïve to get down to work for their exams. No parent wants their own child to accuse them of this kind of neglect.

And parents have even heard the stories of children who actually accused their parents of being too pushy and demanding when they were doing the Leaving Cert., whose self-same children, with the magnificent, selective amnesia of adolescence, have later accused them of not pushing enough. In this seemingly no-win situation, parents are unsure of:

• *What* to do to be helpful.
• *When* such help is needed.
• *How* to intervene in the most effective way.
• When *not* to interfere in case this undermines their child's confidence.
• *How long* to leave a young person to their own devices.

Are They Really Studying?

It hard to know how much study is being done until school exams show the results. In 6th Year that can mean waiting until the results of Christmas exams are sent or even waiting until the Mocks have been completed, at which stage a great deal of crucial time has passed.

Even when children appear to be studying, parents are often unsure whether or not they are really making progress, or whether they might be deluding themselves or their parents into thinking that much more is being achieved than is the case.

Sometimes parents don't know if the positive responses made by their offspring to their queries are simply made to pacify parents that all is under control. Other times they don't know if the angry retorts made to their questions are because the student is coping well and resents the question. Alternatively, could it mean that the student is not coping at all and that the parents' question is an upsetting reminder of that? That is a real worry for parents who are aware that anxiety and depression can express themselves in irritability and anger and withdrawal from help.

Not only that, but parents often find that they no longer know how much to talk to their children about their lives *outside of study and the Leaving Cert.* It seems as if everything gets focused on the Leaving Cert so that the exam silences parents from asking about anything else in the young person's life.

Parents' Dilemma

Of course there are some families who appear to get themselves through the school and exam processes with ease. These are families where the mode of communication seems to combine reasonable parental encouragement with good student application.

But many parents will say that it is impossible to know exactly what their son or daughter wants of them and that, despite parents' best efforts, many conversations about the Leaving Cert. end badly. Each negative conversation can lead to an even more negative exchange, so that it becomes almost taboo to even mention study or exams for fear of an escalation.

What is sad about this is that it means that parents may feel unable to help at a time that their help is actually needed.

Worse, it can leave young people unable to ask for help if they need it at a later stage in the academic year, when a bit of parental support or sympathy might be welcome.

Students' Dilemma

There is often ambivalence in the student's own wishes, which can vacillate over the Leaving Cert. year between a wish for help and a wish to be left alone. On the threshold of adulthood, in that final year of school life, young people often set out in 6th year wanting the respect and responsibility of managing their own study. They believe that they are able to structure, time-manage and keep a balance between work and social life. They want to succeed by their own efforts. They want the dignity of their own decision-making.

But if, despite high motivation, students find that they simply cannot get down to study, then they do need a bit of discreet parental help. They want to be praised for trying. They want sympathy when they struggle. They want encouragement. Most of all they want help when *they* want it, on their terms and only when requested. Although they would also like parents to intuit when help is needed.

Such conflicting demands provide parents with the almost impossible task of meeting the dual request for autonomy and dependence that is a real expression of the developmental struggle between dependence and independence still present in the young adult finishing school.

This needs to be examined so that proper requests and proper responses can replace the confused parent/child communication. Who better to ask than the students and the parents themselves?

What Students Say

The people who can answer best what it is that Leaving Cert. students want from their parents are, of course, Leaving Cert. students.

In order to hear their views, understand their wishes and gain some more insight into what they *do* want from their parents, a sample, of sixty Leaving Cert. students, attending a co-educational second-level institute, were asked this question. They provided their answers in written form in addition to group discussion and elaboration of what they had written.

While this is a small sample and cannot be taken as representative of the total population, it does provide some insight into the views of some Leaving Cert. students.

The major issues identified by the study as being most important to the majority of students were the following:

- Communication with parents.
- Stress and Pressure.
- Social Life.
- Money.

Communication with Parents

One of the important pieces of information to come out of this study is that the majority of the students did not seem to have found an effective channel of communication with their parents.

While viewing their parents as well-intentioned, students found it difficult to negotiate a way of talking to them about the issues that were important to them. When they had tried to do so in the past, the conversations had not provided students with the support they needed. Sometimes, they said, the conversations ended in conflict.

A small number (5 per cent) of the students said that their parents understood them totally and supported them fully, and that they believed that they could get all they needed from their parents. Most did not.

Of course this is *not* to say that 95 per cent of parents were failing. Like most parents, there were things that parents seemed to understand and others that they didn't. The students in this study were quick to identify the positive as well as the negative in what their parents were doing.

What is of particular note is that the majority of the students appreciated their parents' kind intentions even when their parents were 'stressing them out' with their 'help'.

Stress and Pressure

By far the biggest issue for students was this issue of stress or pressure. While students spoke about this in a variety of ways, using phrases of advice to their parents such as *'back off'*, *'stop stressing me out'*, *'ease up the pressure'* or *'stop wrecking my head'*, the message was clear. It was that students were primarily experiencing their parents' interventions in relation to the Leaving Cert. as stressful.

Students said that what their parents' thought was supportive was often experienced by the student as additional pressure. This particularly pertained to questions about study progress and the manner in which these questions were asked. While many students recognised that parental questions were motivated by interest and concern, the students' experience of these questions was that they caused them further pressure. They said they wished their parents would stop asking them questions because they never knew how to answer them and because it didn't help.

Some students said that pressure came more from school than from home. They complained about the lack of coordination between teachers with regard to homework. It seemed that students often found themselves having to produce major homework assignments in the same week for a number of individual teachers followed by a week when there was minimal homework. Those who mentioned this work overload said they were exceptionally stressed by it.

But apart from any conversations with parents, or indeed, with teachers, the inherent pressure and stress to study and to succeed in the Leaving Cert. exam was a significant issue for the majority of students.

Social Life

The next major issue raised by the students related to social life. Going out with friends was described as one of the most important ways of coping with pressure. Students said that their parents did not appear to appreciate the important stress-reduction role going out and meeting friends played in their lives. Some said that parents were okay at the beginning of the year, but expected them to stay at home once the exams were getting near. Some 20 per cent of the students specifically named going out with friends as the main source of conflict between them and their parents.

Allied to this, students spoke about the need to keep in contact with friends after school by phone, either on their home line or mobile phone. Almost two-thirds of students in this group stated that they had mobile phones, although they were often out of credit or low in credit. Texting their friends was, therefore, a more economical contact method. It was the most frequent means by which students maintained contact with each other, particularly when making arrangements to meet.

If they could not meet their friends, students said that it helped them if they could phone them from a home landline or text them on their mobile phones.

Money

The next most frequently raised issue by the students was the issue of money. Most students said that they needed more money. Students spoke about the difference between parents' perception of the cost of living and the students' day-to-day expenses.

Some students joked about how out of touch their parents were with the cost of living. Others were stressed trying to manage on what they perceived as inadequate amounts and said that their parents did not seem to realise that giving them bus money and lunch money was not giving them pocket money. A few said that their parents did not seem to know how miserable and anxious they felt when they were short of money. It was also an embarrassment with their friends if they could not pay their way.

A number of students solved the money problem by taking jobs. It is interesting that the Youthscape Survey (Ireland.com 2000) shows that by the time they are seventeen years old more than half of all teenage males work.

But there were some students in this study who felt unable to cope with the pressure of paid work, school and study. Some specifically wished that they would not have to earn money, and said that they wanted to give up their jobs, particularly in the weeks prior to the exams.

Disappointing Parents

There were some students whose primary concern was about hurting or disappointing their parents. They said that they could usually tell if their parents were disappointed, even when their parents tried to hide it. Disappointing their parents appeared to be an issue for the majority of students. This was a particular worry for students who were *repeating* the Leaving Cert.

Most of the students who were repeating stated that they felt disappointed in themselves. They also said that they felt they had disappointed their parents, although this tended to depend on how well they had done the first time. There was a difference between those who had achieved well, but insufficiently for a particular chosen course or college place, and those who had got very low points or had 'failed' in certain subjects. The latter were more anxious.

Parental Expectations

There did not seem to be too big a difference in students' minds between trying 'not to disappoint their parents' and trying 'to live up to parental expectations'.

Ironically, if parents placed too much trust in a student's ability, having high expectations of that student, students said that this was almost as stressful as low expectations or poor trust in the student's capacity. The recommendation from students was that parents would trust them to *do their best* and be pleased with that rather than focusing on results.

Praise and Encouragement

Students also spoke about the need for praise and recognition for studying. They felt that praise was very important and it meant a lot to them when their parents praised them or when they were sympathetic towards them. Some felt that their parents either did not see or did not acknowledge the effort they were putting in to their studies.

There was no consensus about how parents *could* acknowledge this, although letting them out with their friends or being generous with money to go out with their friends after a hard stint of study were suggested.

A few students suggested that their parents might simply tell them they noticed how hard they were studying.

False Reassurances

Students found it difficult when their expressions of anxiety were met with an immediate parental 'reassurance' that they would be 'fine'. This response was experienced as negating the students' worry.

While this did not feature in the top three issues identified by the students, it does feature very high on the list of unhelpful things a parent can say.

Other Students' Points

The following information also emerged from the study:

- Students highlighted their parents' role in the Leaving Cert., both as people who support them and people who stress them.

- The actual stress, which students spoke about, took many forms. Some described it as feeling 'frantic' with worry. Others used the term 'scared'. Some said it changed, sometimes being acute, at other times being manageable. Still others spoke about stress as being more ongoing and part of the day-to-day pressure of being in 6th year.
- Some said they wanted their parents to appreciate how often they felt caught between pressure from the school and pressure from home, identifying those situations as being the most difficult.
- Only two students out of sixty believed that they needed their parents to 'hassle' them into study. For the majority, coercion was a deterrent to study. Not only that, but if a parent suggested study when a student had already planned to do so, this even stopped the student from studying on the basis that the parent would now believe that the only reason the student was studying was because the parent had demanded it.
- A small number of students (5 per cent) said they were angry with their parents for 'freaking out' about the results of their Christmas exams or Mocks, and wanted to remind their parents that none of these results were the actual Leaving Cert. and that there was time to improve.
- With regard to expectations, students were upset if parents had too high a belief in the student's capacity. They were also upset if expectations were too low, with not enough trust that the student was working.
- Some students who felt they had the situation under control would have liked their parents' recognition of this.
- A small number of students rated their parents as more stressed than they, the students, were.
- A few students said they had difficulty with noise levels at home from younger brothers and sisters.
- A few students were very specific and said that it would be nice to come home to a warm welcome, a hot meal and some of their favourite foods during exam time.

Summary of Students' Views

The key message from students was that they had not yet found an effective channel of communication with their parents. Students also wanted their parents to know that they were doing their best, that they were feeling stressed and that going out with their friends was an important way of relaxing. Additionally, that having the money to do so was important to them.

While the majority of students recognised their parents' good intentions, parents and students did not yet have a productive way of talking to each other about study. Indeed, many students suggested that parents 'back off' with their queries about study while acknowledging the importance of having their parents support them in other ways.

Students also suggested more expressions of sympathy and understanding from their parents about how stressful their lives were.

Points for Parents

What may be interesting for parents reading this, if they are not already aware of it, is how important it is to students to have a good relationship with their parents, how much emphasis they place on parental approbation, how aware they are of disappointing their parents and how stressed the majority of students feel during the year. Also, how important it is for students to find a way of communicating more effectively with their parents throughout the year.

So what can a parent do? If, as the study shows, parents and students have not found an effective channel of communication with each other, then one thing that can most certainly be done is for parents to experiment with alternative means of connecting with their children.

Snail-Mail

One means of communicating with young people that is very effective is writing *to them*. This is a greatly under-utilised, but powerful, method of communication. It provides a way of acknowledging how stressful the year is for students and an opportunity to ask them what kind of help they would like. It is also an opportunity to praise and encourage students, since students identified that as being important to them.

There are also arrays of cards for sale with supportive messages that can supplement a letter, if appropriate. There are cards that offer support, cards that let someone know that the writer of the card cares, cards that state that if help is needed the card-sender is available. There are blank cards on to which any message can be written. There are even cards that acknowledge that this is a difficult time for the recipient of the card. Parents can, therefore, choose from an array of messages or create their own way of telling the young person that they are behind them all the way.

Email

In households lucky enough to have PCs and email, parents can also email their children. An email from a parent with a chirpy message can help to lighten the mood for a student on their return home from school or at the beginning of a study session. Even a message that says *'there'll be a cup of tea and biscuits waiting downstairs at 9.30 if you're taking a break'* can be a fun way of keeping up a light-hearted connection with the student.

Text

Of course the ultimate communication medium for students who have mobile phones is sending text messages. Having text appear from a parent, such as 'r u ok?' is a great surprise.

Adolescents are sometimes amazed to find that their parents have broken the adolescent text code, so to speak. Certainly this is a way of sending simple supportive messages or genuine queries to young people. They are the masters of technology; sometimes we need to access their world, if we wish to access them.

Advantage for Students

The advantage of parents communicating with their adolescent children in any of the above ways is that:

- They will certainly 'receive' the message.
- The novelty may take them by surprise.
- They have time to read the message and absorb it. And reread it.
- They cannot divert the topic to another.
- They cannot dismiss the sentiment or protest that they are 'fine' and need no help.
- They do not have to hide how pleased they are.
- They do not have to answer at all if they choose not to.
- They can retain the sympathetic words to help them through a bleak time.

Advantages for Parents

The advantages for parents of these modes of communication, over and above the usual parent/child discussions are the following:

- Parents can take their time and select their words carefully in a way that conveys exactly their message of care and concern.
- Even if a message is a tricky one, in which a parent needs to let a student know that they are worried that the student

seems unable to study, this can be a carefully crafted message. It can begin with an account of all the wonderful things the parent observes in their child and then move gently to express the parents' worry that 6th year is proving difficult. It can finish with an offer of help.

- It is, of course, important that parents' communications identify the positive behaviours that parents have observed. Also that nothing upsetting to the student is put in writing.
- Praise is *never* wasted. A sympathetic recognition that this is a hard time for the student is always appreciated. This can be followed by a light-hearted invitation to the student to let parents know how they could be helpful and supportive during the rest of the year.

Finally, a sentence that reminds children how much they are loved is exceptionally reassuring for the tired or stressed student.

6

TIME MANAGEMENT

Time management is time well spent. It is crucial in 6th year. A year goes very quickly. Without a clear plan and a timetable the whole Leaving Cert. enterprise can go decidedly wrong.

With less than forty weeks from September to June, wasted time is lost time. A simple calculation shows that a student taking seven subjects in the Leaving Cert. exam has *less than six weeks per subject* between day one back at school and day one of the Leaving Cert. exam. Factor out Christmas Holidays, Mid-Term Break, Halloween, Easter and other special events and the number of weeks per subject decreases drastically.

Parents know this. They know how short an academic year is and how quickly it flies by. This is because they have the mature capacity to plan, prioritise, anticipate and make realistic judgments about what is involved. Faced with the challenge of a time-specific, time-limited project, such as the Leaving Cert., most adults can calculate realistically what needs to be done. And it kills them when their children won't do this.

Leaving Cert. students usually have a completely different notion of time to their parents. They hold different views on what time of the day is early or late, depending on the activity in which they are engaging. They have utterly different perceptions of the time required to get somewhere and even less, parents say, of the time it takes to get home.

And let's face it, when you are young, enthusiastic and exuberant, when the world is exciting and you are full of life, time does seem to stretch endlessly before you. This is why the parental alarm-clock calls, so to speak, to study and duty and responsibility, are so often ignored.

It is not that the Leaving Cert. student does not listen, at all, to what is said about time. It is simply that many of them genuinely do not realise the time constraints under which they operate. A year seems like a lifetime and there are always great intentions to get down to the study next week.

Time-Management Difficulties

What the Research Says
What many people do *not* realise, when they despair of young people, is that these capacities, planning, organising, anticipating, judging and decision-making often do not come to maturity until early adulthood.

Recent research in Harvard and elsewhere has given important understanding of why so many adolescents are chronically disorganised, untidy, scatty and unrealistic at times. This research is worth explaining in a little detail.[1]

It would seem that there are profound changes in the part of the brain known as the frontal lobes[2] during adolescence. For example, to carry out a task we must do a number of things, plan in advance and select what we are going to do from a wide variety of options. Because we often only have a certain amount of time for the task we have to ignore other things and just keep to the work in hand. Finally, as we come to the end of a task we have to keep track of what we have already done.

These different components, setting goals, planning, carrying out goal-directed plans and effective performance all require adolescents to behave in particular ways that are not fully developed until adulthood. Research shows that problems in these executive functions are connected to frontal lobe damage. The research is also showing that this is an area of the brain that is not fully developed until adulthood.

SURVIVING THE LEAVING CERT.

New technology now allows us to look at the brain as it is working on a task. Pictures of the brain appear on the screen and parts of the brain 'light up' so that we can see what parts of the brain are being used when we do specific things

The 'Harvard' research using the technology of FMRI (functional magnetic resonance imaging) special brain scans of the brain in action, showed that precisely those parts of the brain associated with planning, organising, anticipating, judging and decision-making,[3] even interpreting the emotions in their parents' faces are still relatively immature in the majority of adolescents. This so called neurobiological and neuropsychological research is important in helping us understand young people.

These are *genuine* difficulties, for which there has, perhaps, been insufficient sympathy for students when they have been distracted, impulsive, shown poor insight and poor control. The perennial cry of parents to offspring to *'grow up'* or *'act their age'* might be more a response to the dynamic adolescent brain than to the difficult adolescent person.

And the complaint of parents that their children are *'so immature'* or *'wired to the moon'* is precisely because the brain wiring and rewiring is still incomplete.

Think of the frustration parents feel when they get a ridiculous response to a reasonable argument about needing to plan ahead. When there seems to be no insight whatsoever that days and weeks are rushing by and still no study plan or pattern has been formulated. When the tiniest external cue distracts the adolescent from study. And when the student's reception to advice about time-management and formulating study plans meets with a less than gratifying reception.

As in all situations there will of course be different levels of maturity in individual young people and for a variety of reasons some will already be much better in planning and organising than others. But it may be reassuring for parents to know that time should unravel many of their worries, that maturity is on the horizon and that in the meantime some practical, discreet support to help the student get organised may be the best use of their energy.

Once we know that something is beyond a person's immediate control it is easier to be sympathetic and practically helpful. This is not to remove all responsibility from the student for managing their studies, but to help students to learn how to take responsibility for their studies, what they need to do to manage their time, to organise themselves. Also how to seek help and accept help in these important management tasks.

The Time 'Mismanager'

If there is overall immaturity in the time-management and planning circuitry of younger people, this obviously still varies from one person to the next, with some students being reasonably organised and others cripplingly, chronically disorganised.

Students who have especial difficulty managing study time are highly identifiable because their organisational and time-management difficulties often spill over into many other areas of their lives. Parents will have no difficulty knowing and recognising these signs as they themselves are so often frustrated and exhausted by the number of reminders they have to issue about routine events.

Disorganised Students
The following are some of the difficulties experienced by the chronically disorganised students:

- They may be at the wrong place at the wrong time. In school they may turn up for the wrong class or activity.
- They may be uncertain exactly where they are meant to be because they have not consulted their timetable or diary.
- Tidiness may be a problem.
- Belongings may be lost on a frequent basis.
- In instances where the homework assignment has been completed, the notebook, copy or folder in which it is

contained may have been left at home or forgotten.

- Alternatively, the homework assignment may be incomplete because the student ran out of time or mistook the day on which it was due to be handed in.
- Notes may be in disarray, so that large sheaves of paper may be pulled from the school bag or stuffed into it at the end of the day. With each week the number of papers increases and the task of sorting them becomes more difficult.
- Without a proper, organised folder for each subject, or filing system for each topic, notes can go missing, get inadvertently thrown out or become too crumpled to be legible.
- When attempting to study, students may end up missing large chunks of information because all the notes relating to a particular subject are not filed together.
- Students may not have the required books with them in class.
- There may be a tendency to forget PE gear, sports clothes, hockey sticks, tennis rackets, rugby boots or, indeed, whatever is required for the school sporting activity.
- Alternatively the wrong sports gear may be brought because of a confusion about which sports activity occurs on which day.
- Because of poor punctuality, the student may miss the start of class. This puts the student in the position of spending much of the remainder of the class trying to catch up with what is happening. If the class is a maths class in which a new concept has been introduced, then the student may begin that maths section disadvantaged.

Psychological Effects

Not only are there practical day-to-day consequences of being able, or unable, to manage time, but ability in this area, allied to other factors in the young person's life, can bring about either positive or negative psychological experiences.

Psychological Problems

There are significant psychological difficulties for the student who watches days, weeks and months slip by in disarray. The disorganised student is likely to become overwhelmed and immobilised by worries about what has to be done, or by the belief that there is no time left to do it. This, in itself is a significant source of stress.

The following are some of the psychological problems that arise for the student who cannot prioritise, plan and manage time:

- Punctuality is often an ongoing problem. Rushing late to activities induces stress. This stress further inhibits the capacity to concentrate, organise and remember, plunging the student into a vicious cycle of difficulty.
- Procrastination is perfected and everything associated with study is deferred to 'tomorrow'.
- Other avoidance strategies may be adopted. Sometimes students who have run out of excuses somatise their problems. These excuses, based on physical complaints and illness, may be useful ways of avoiding the wrath of authority figures and, in this insidious way, a dangerous negative pattern of task avoidance can begin.
- Stress occurs as the exams approach and as students feel increasingly unable to apply themselves to study. Students may then fritter away the remaining available time in increased worry and end up engaging in distracted, disorganised and distressing attempts to catch up.
- Depression tends to be associated with feelings of poor self-esteem, of worthlessness, helplessness and hopelessness. These set in when students feel that they have lost control over their lives, when they feel that too many demands are being made of them or when they feel increasingly unable to meet those demands. If this should happen it needs to be taken seriously.
- Panicky feelings may occur. Panic further reduces the capacity of students to manage their time.

- Sleep may be disturbed as they become increasingly worried and upset and of course this in turn makes memory, particularly short-term memory worse.
- In some instances an acute anxiety episode or a panic attack may occur as exams approach for which a student feels ill prepared.
- At this stage fear of having a panic attack may significantly disable a student psychologically.

Students suffering psychological distress as a result of feeling overwhelmed by the pressure of the exams or their inability to organise themselves need all the help, understanding and support they can get.

If there is any suspicion of extreme stress, panic attacks or depression professional help should be sought.

Psychological Benefits

If there are psychological difficulties for the time-mismanaged student, there are significant benefits for those who have more maturity in this capacity.

Students who can organise, plan and maximise learning opportunities in 6th Year usually feel in control of study and can measure their own progress, their study, revision and exam-preparation time in the course of the year. This increases self-esteem, provides confidence, reduces stress and may prevent the student from feeling daunted by study tasks.

Time management is not just about managing time, but is often symptomatic of a life-style approach, which carries enormous psychological benefits. Amongst the more significant benefits for the student who can manage time or who accepts the help of their parents or their teachers to do so are the following:

- Tasks are prioritised so the important ones are completed. This provides a great sense of confidence and control to the student.

- Parental relationships are likely to be good, as parents observe the students' management of study and other activities.
- Relationships with teachers are also usually favourable as homework assignments are completed, well-presented and handed in on time.
- Stress is reduced. The student is not racing from one catastrophe to the next. Instead the student has the perception of being able to cope.
- Self-esteem is good. There is less likelihood of panic as a schedule of study reassures that the subjects *can* be covered.

The Time-Managed Family

The first step to effective time-management is to believe that managing time is important. Some families do this naturally. Others do not.

There are families that are utterly chaotic, where most events happen because of last-minute crisis mobile-phone calls. There are families who are extraordinarily organised, so that each moment is accounted for and each family member works to this programme. Provided there is flexibility and the schedules are not tense, rigid, punitive or obsessive these structures can provide security for children and adolescents.

Then there are the many families who have eventually devised schedules by learning painfully that the only way to coordinate the myriad needs and multiple activities of many different people within the family is to get organised. Different family members may have differing capacity, but the overall running of the household is reasonably efficient.

But whatever the family style, children are always aware of it, even if they don't always actively participate in it. For this reason, the example shown by parents is a major factor in how young people plan and organise their own lives in the following ways:

- Students who observe their parents create lists, prioritise tasks and plan ahead will already have been inducted into the relevance of organisation.
- They may note that if being organised does not come naturally then it has to be worked at and it can be achieved.
- While young people will always protest at the nuisance of having to do things NOW rather than *later*, or *tomorrow*, being trained to attend to what is immediate does help their own organisational capacities when left to their own devices.
- The relationship between disorganisation and stress is observed. Students notice that time-management strategies operated in the home reduce stress for everyone.
- They also observe the practical benefits: if the breakfast table is set the night before rather than the rush for cups and cutlery in the morning. Having all bags, books or objects to be taken to school the next day left at the hall door, so that they will not be forgotten brings a better start to the school day than the rush and rummaging in the laundry basket for PE gear.
- Students are alerted to the benefit of tidiness in their own study space, the value of discarding the accumulation of clutter. They note that it is important to empty wastebaskets, remove coffee cups, sweet and snack wrappers and rubbish from the study area and how this assists in keeping a semblance of order on the study process.

Time Management and Sleep

Students need sufficient sleep[4] in order to feel well and feel in control of their study. All time-management schedules should factor in an understanding of the persons' energy patterns and sleep patterns. Realistic account need to be taken of rest and sleep time when elaborate study tables are being made. Students should, therefore be encouraged to:

- Establish the time of day at which study is most effective. Some people are larks, others are owls, that is, those who work best early or those who study best late at night. What is important is to know when a student's peak energy time is during the day and what pattern is most useful during this life stage. Late hours do not fit well with early school days.

- Students who enter into debate with their parents about staying up late often quote the many famous night owls such as Edison, Dostoevsky, Pascal and Byron. Parents may quote back a few famous larks such as Milton and Schubert and Schopenhauer. None of these were doing the Leaving Cert. What the student needs to remember is that many exams are scheduled for the morning. A pattern of late night study does not fit well with early morning exams.

- Students also cannot burn the candle at both ends. Research at Boston's Harvard Medical School, which was reported on in 2000 in the journal *Nature Neuroscience,* shows that people need to sleep within hours of learning a new task or their performance on the task is impaired. In one study if students did not get sleep until twenty-one hours or more after learning, their performance was severely impaired. It is suggested that the sleep obtained after learning is critical for wiring new information into the brain.

- Other research shows the memory inefficiencies that arise with less than seven hours sleep in the younger brain. Material learned late at night will not be retrieved easily if the student has less than seven hours sleep.

- Additionally a 1998 study[5] showed that students who received low grades went to bed forty minutes later on school nights than students with high grades and that adolescents who slept less than seven hours reported increased daytime sleepiness and other problems including depressed mood.

- Students, should, therefore, try to have sufficient sleep. In addition to the amount of sleep it is also important to have uninterrupted sleep. An Italian study[6] reported on in 2000 in the journal *Behavioural Brain Research* shows that people can remember what they studied the night before if they can have *uninterrupted* sleep. Unless a student has to share a bedroom, it might be best to provide the quietest sleeping arrangements for the student during the Leaving Cert. year.

Does Your Child Need Help with Time Management?

Points For Parents
If, as the research tells us, there is immaturity in adolescents' capacity to manage time, plan and organise, then they *do* need help in these important processes. Parents, who have good organisational capacity *and* patience, can do a number of things to help the young person by inviting them to do the following:

- Set aside a specific notebook or diary for daily lists of tasks and longer-term study plans. Enter the occasions that are already known, such as birthdays and family events.
- Social events, time out with friends at weekends should be noted.
- Plan daily tasks rather than distant achievements.
- Prioritise tasks so that the most important always gets done.
- Make a list of things that must be done, things one would like to do and things that can wait if necessary.
- Make use of every moment. Students often think that they can only study if they have set aside a long stretch of time. This is not so and there are important small clusters of time that can be put to excellent use. Identify any such time that could be used but that is currently being wasted e.g. waiting at a bus stop, waiting for dinner in the evening. These minutes can add up to hours over a few weeks.
- Consider how to use small time-spaces. Carrying around a small pocket dictionary or thesaurus can be an excellent way of improving vocabulary or increasing one's understanding of words.

- Alternatively use this time to learn grammar or verbs in the Leaving Cert. foreign language chosen. Pocket editions are discreet and convenient.
- Set realistic goals. The goal is not to do brilliantly in the Leaving Cert. The goal is to study *today*.
- Do task analysis. Determine what has to be done within a specified period and then how to break up the task into realistic sub-tasks.
- Remind the student about how much time is lost after late nights out or after excessive use of alcohol. Research done in 2000 shows that alcohol affects adolescents differently to adults because of the many changes in the brain that are now known to be occurring during this time. This research suggests that adolescents may be more vulnerable than adults to the effects of alcohol on their learning abilities and their memory and on their developing brain.
- Apart from specific difficulties associated with alcohol, as the Leaving Cert. year progresses the lateness of social time and the use of alcohol in social time requires some attention from the student.
- Students are advised to set aside a time in the evening for phone calls. It is important not to make or receive calls outside this time. This is a point that cannot be made too often, as it is a crucial time-consumer in students' lives. If withdrawal is acute, incoming messages can be read or listened to. At least that will be at one time, preferably as a reward after a forty-minute studying session.
- End each day by reviewing the list of study tasks and how many were achieved. Note any patterns. Was the list too long, unrealistic, were some priority tasks continuously shifted down the list and not attended to? What does the list tell the student about study patterns, success and difficulties.
- Take *time* to reflect on the great privilege it is to be a student. While it may be hard to go through the Leaving Cert. year, there are many people who never had that opportunity and who grieved the loss of an education.

Parents may feel that they themselves are being deprived of their own personal time while they devote so much to the student. However, early support in understanding and managing time has been found to bring about changes in how students approach their work.

Also, the student who is unable to respond to your help may not be ready for the responsibilities of the Leaving Cert. in which case expectations may need to be adjusted to highly realistic levels. Sometimes parents become so frustrated by the student who appears to be unable or unwilling to comply with any suggestions for learning, organising and time-management. If that is so and the student is not developmentally ready it may be better to establish that early on rather than jeopardise the parent-child relationship by putting undue pressure on someone who is not yet ready or able to respond.

Parents and students need to find their own way of talking about study. This is not always an easy thing to do because of the degree of emotion that each has invested in the enterprise.

Negotiating the balance between routine and relaxation, and between alerting the student to the realities of time without panicking the student about the constraints of time, is indeed, a challenge for parents.

And timing is everything.

Notes

1 Research by Dr Deborah Yurgelun-Todd, Ph.D., Harvard Medical School, Boston MA.

2 Frontal lobes, in which there are many regions associated with different skills. If these areas are damaged or not fully developed you can get problem behaviour. For example, disease or injury in the prefrontal regions can cause problems in behaviour and personality, with poor decision-making, risk-taking, impulsivity and misreading emotions.

3 Baird, A.A., Gruber, S.A., Cohen, B.M., Renshaw, P.F., Steincard, R. J., Yurgelin-Todd, D.A. (1999) 'FMRI of the amygdala in children and adolescents.' *Journal of American Child and Adolescent Psychiatry* 38 (2) 195-99.

4 Murray, M. (1994) 'Sleep Problems' in Keane, C. (ed) (1994), *Nervous Breakdown*, Mercier Press, Cork.

5 Wolfson, A. (1998) *Child Development,* Vol. 69 (4) 875-887.

6 Ficca, G. et al (2000) *Behavioural Brain Research,* Vol. 112 (12) 159-163.

7

PROCRASTINATION

What is Procrastination?

Procrastination is the thief of time. It is the greatest enemy of the Leaving Cert. student. It is the ultimate in unconscious delaying tactics. It has the power to sabotage any project if we do not know how to tackle it.

Parents watching students procrastinate often marvel at their capacity to accomplish so little with so much effort in so much time.

These performances in the definitive art of distractibility often convince parents that it would be easier to sit the Leaving Cert. themselves than witness the diversionary antics of the student.

When the student has appeared for the fifth time in an hour for a quick snack, in search of a pen or just to watch a few minutes TV, then parents know that it would be easier to tackle the exam than the adolescent.

Sometimes procrastination is another expression of anxiety and fear. Beginning to study can initially raise these emotions as the student confronts the reality of all that has to be done.

Putting off study feels like putting off the fear, except that it doesn't work. What actually happens is that the fear builds up, the guilt seeps in, the next study attempt is harder and the next deferral swifter.

To alleviate guilt student sometimes rationalise that they cannot study until they have done other things. These can be any study related activities, such as tidying tidy desks, sorting school books on shelves, photocopying notes, sharpening pencils, even making time-tables. Procrastination compounds itself so that everything else gets done. Everything *but* study.

And herein lies the ultimate diagnostic tool for procrastination; if the activity has got to do with study but is *never actual study* then it is procrastination.

Forms of Procrastination

There is no limit to the creative procrastination capacities of adolescents. Sometimes procrastination is a symptom of time-management problems.

After all, if there is no plan, if you don't know what you are meant to know, how to begin, where to begin, how to plan a night's study, what subject to study, or how to track and record your progress at the end, then it seems easier to decide to begin another time.

Parents are very familiar with adolescents' procrastinating proficiency, which often takes the following forms:

- Making endless lists of tasks and elaborate timetables, which do not appear to get implemented.
- Resolving to study tomorrow, next week, after some particular event, or even next term.
- Making time-consuming mobile calls to friends to get social arrangements 'out of the way' before getting down to study.
- Deciding to watch just one TV programme before beginning study. Then deciding to watch 'an educational TV' programme that could help with study.
- Having another snack to fortify for the work ahead.
- Rationalising that all these things must be done first in order to study.
- Even when the student is eventually sitting in front of the books, the tasks get extended to ruling neat margins,

numbering pages, switching from textbook to textbook and subject to subject, before eventually leaving the room for further nutritional supplies.

Consequences for the Student

Students do not intentionally sabotage themselves to this extent. In fact they usually begin the evening with good intentions, high motivation and firm determination to put in a good night's work. As the time goes by, many students feel increasingly worthless as they 'put in the hours' with no visible achievement or personal sense of having learned anything.

Even homework assignments, which can help to combat procrastination, because there is a specified task and a due date for delivery, can fall behind schedule as the student's sense of competence disappears. The contagion of poor confidence spills into every task.

Additionally, most students will admit that they carry the worry from one activity to the next, so that in the end they don't know where to begin at all. Often the so-called 'diversionary' activities are an expression of anxiety, in which the student leaves the books rather than tackle the difficult maths problem, the incomprehensible text and the fears of failure that they evoke.

This is why students who talk about the procrastination experience often describe a range of emotions. These descriptions tend to include words and phrases such as *'frustration, anger, feeling inadequate, feeling stupid, worrying about concentration'*. This may cause them to become stressed, anxious and overwhelmed and in some instances even to opt out of the entire exam process.

Furthermore, students who find themselves repeatedly and increasingly having difficulty in following a study plan, have no way of tracking their progress or of feeling in control of their work. Because of this they often come to believe that they are not intellectually or academically capable when, in fact, their difficulty is one of not knowing how to study.

This requires parental sympathy and help.

How Can a Parent Help?

Some parents react with anger at what they perceive to be unnecessary delaying tactics. Others express sympathy towards the student, recognising that the good intentions are being dissipated in futile exercises after which the student is probably even more exhausted than would have been the case if uninterrupted, concentrated study had taken place.

Most parents say that they are frustrated and concerned as they watch valuable days and weeks disappear. Certainly, any parent witnessing their child's procrastination would like to help. The following points may be useful:

- Unless you are having a particularly difficult time with an adolescent who is intentionally being oppositional in many areas, chances are that this behaviour is out of the adolescent's control.
- Recognise the behaviour for what it is, a sign of difficulty rather than a sign of defiance. This is not to say that adolescents will not react irritably or even with incredulity if challenged. However, this is often because of their personal anxiety in the situation. Sometimes it is even an indication of their own lack of insight about how little they are accomplishing.
- Remind yourself that these unproductive activities carry no benefit for students. It would of course be easier for them to do their homework, engage in some extra study and then be in a position to relax if they could do so. If there is no logic to the behaviour or apparent benefit for the adolescent then this can be a sign that it is a problem with which they need help.
- Provide some strategies to help them. For example, routine is a great antidote to procrastination. Arrange for dinner at a specific time and for the student to begin study immediately

afterwards. Setting the study time-clock helps to develop a more positive pattern.

- Suggest that they begin the evening with *just fifteen minutes study*. Point out that all other activities can wait for fifteen minutes. Often, just getting promptly into study without the anxious or deferring rituals can help the student not only to begin, but also to stay there.
- Explain that starting to study is like the initial plunge into cold water for a swim. The body takes a few minutes to adjust, but once in the sea, the water gets warmer.
- Encourage the student to use some of the simple time-management strategies. An example would be to make a *short* list of two to three items – not an elaborate timetable that takes hours to create – of what exactly the student is going to study. If this is task specific, with very small initial tasks e.g. read a poem, do pages 50-54 in Geography then it is more likely to be done.
- Suggest that the student, who still cannot study, make a list of every activity and every distraction. For example they should document every phone call, every trip away from the study room, every TV programme watched etc. Sometimes recognising the pattern of distractibility can help a student to adjust it.
- Offer to help by calling in to the student at 30-40 minute intervals. It is nice to call a student down for a cup of tea or a snack that you have prepared. This is a sign of sympathy and encouragement.
- Offer to help with phone calls either by telling friends the student won't be available until a certain time. Alternatively arrange with the student that they make and receive calls between certain hours. Phone calls from friends can be particularly distracting. If they are about social arrangements, afterwards the study room can seem so boring and prison-like. This point cannot be made too often because phone calls are one of the biggest distractions for adolescent students.
- Invite the student to undertake a particular piece of study and then to explain it to you. Study that has a focus is more

effective. Also we learn and retain better what we have to explain to another person.

- Suggest that students select the TV programmes they would like to watch in advance. Agree to call them for the programme so that further valuable time is not wasted checking time, checking to see if it has begun or watching ads.
- When the TV programme ends it is helpful if parents are around to turn off the TV. This helps the student leave the room, otherwise the temptation will be to watch just a few minutes of another programme and many a night's study can end this way.
- Alternatively, some students get a supply of videotapes and tape their favourite programmes. This means that the programmes can be watched at the end of the evening and serve as a reward for study done.
- Suggest that the student make a list of everything studied. This can give a sense of competence and achievement. It is encouraging to see the list grow.
- If there is something particularly exciting happening in the household that the student would like to be part of, it is probably better to advise the night off than have it wasted anyway in unproductive and frustrating attempts at study. This can add to students' burnout if they feel they always have to be on study call.
- Remind the student that the brain is programmable. It can be programmed to study. It can be programmed to study for specified periods, beginning with 20 minutes, increasing to 30 minutes and finally 40 minute stretches which is about the optimal amount of time to study without a break. It is akin to fitness training. Begin slowly and realistically and build up to brainpower.
- Remind the student how good it feels to take a break after productive study.
- Look out for signs of anxiety in the student. Suggest that instead of thinking ahead, it is often better to focus on what has to be done today.

- Help them to see that the best way to reduce anxiety about study is to study and that the best way to get down to study is to study.

Finally, if your child is in difficulty with procrastination and you want to help, don't put it off.
Do it today!

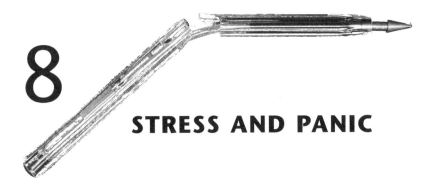

8

STRESS AND PANIC

People sometimes panic as the Leaving Cert. approaches. Suddenly there seems to be no time left to do anything and everything left to be done.

Deadliners

Of course the adrenalin produced by the realisation that time is running out can help some students to finally focus their efforts and concentrate on their studies. These students are the ones who only get working when there is a visible deadline that is fast approaching. Often these are the adrenalin addicts who like to get close to the wire before they get down to it, or who even rely on the wire to jolt them into action.

Perfectionists

Perfectionists can also leave things late. This is because in striving for perfection there is an attempt to cover each item on the curriculum meticulously. Total control is an impossible goal, which cannot be met. It often immobilises those who aspire to it.

Ironically, as the exam approaches, perfectionists may be liberated from this need for perfection and realise that they have to do what is possible. The deadline provides the perfectionist with permission, so to speak, to make a more realistic appraisal of what can be done, to strategise and to concentrate.

How to relinquish the impossible in order to achieve the attainable is an important life lesson.

Worriers

But there are those other students in whom deadlines induce a terrible and incapacitating sense of panic. They feel that it is futile to try to catch up at such a late stage. Overtaken by fear of failure, they may become frantic to do everything at once. They may find themselves opening one book and abandoning it, changing to another subject and discarding that, deciding that they should really work on yet another subject, which in turn gets set aside. They become anxious when they study and more anxious when they do not, an experience that is utterly overwhelming in itself.

Workers

And it is not only students who have not prepared sufficiently who can feel overwhelmed. The highly conscientious student can begin to worry about whether all their hard work will pay off. This can be an even greater stress. Whatever about getting ones' justifiable deserts for not studying, it is infinitely worse to work hard and fail. Think of the humiliation. To have everyone *know* that you have studied exhaustively, to have had your parents praise and boast about how hard you have worked, and then to *fail*. This can seem like an even greater catastrophe.

Developers

Some students are not sufficiently mature when the reach 6th year to do what is required of them at that life stage. They have not developed sufficiently emotionally, academically or personally. They have not learned to take on a challenge. They do not have the capacity, yet, to manage their time and no amount of help seems to get them started. They do not have career aspirations for which the Leaving Cert. seems relevant. They are either not able to work or not willing to work. Unwillingness to try is a psychological disability.

In this situation, it is often preferable to regard the year as a year of great learning for student and parent. Sometimes students have to discover that there are goals that cannot be bought for them, work that cannot be removed from them and achievements that can only be got by their own efforts. If they fail the Leaving Cert., or do badly, then they will have to learn to deal with failure. They will have to examine their capabilities and try again.

Whether or not this student becomes stressed is unpredictable. What is important is that the parents of this student do not become stressed out trying to force the impossible on the unwilling.

You cannot do it for them. They cannot do it for themselves yet. They are not ready.

What Makes It Stressful?

Regardless of the type of student a young person is, there are real, objective and undeniable stressors attached to the Leaving Cert. Those living or working with young people are rightly concerned about the levels of stress many of them experience in relation to the Leaving Cert. and how they deal with that stress.

Consider the following.

- The Leaving Cert. is an exam at the end of a person's school life.
- It is spoken and written about as if it were the ultimate marker of a person's worth.
- It receives enormous media attention. Weeks of airwave advice are devoted to it, particularly as the exam approaches. There are daily programmes about specific examination subjects, in addition to advice about physical and psychological preparation for the event.
- There are news items and newspaper articles when the results are published about those students who achieved almost maximum points.
- Parents have invested time, money, energy and concern in their success.
- If the student is repeating, this may be in an expensive private situation.

- All their family, friends and relations will receive the student's results in detail.
- Comparisons are made with siblings, relations and friends.
- The Leaving Cert. results dictate whether or not a person gets their third-level choice or a coveted college place.
- It may determine the jobs for which a student is eligible.
- It appears to the student to be the most important and ultimate determiner of a student's future.

This is the context in which young people set out to undertake the exam. It is not surprising, therefore, that some students get stressed and panicked as the exam approaches.

A student who is struggling intellectually or academically with a subject will experience stress. Students who opt for the higher level in subjects in which they have no aptitude will be stressed.

Students with the challenges posed by a specific learning difficulty will feel stressed, depending on what arrangements have been made to facilitate them. If they have been awarded special consideration, such as extra time, use of a reader, a word processor or a scribe or amanuensis to whom they can dictate answers, they will feel better.

Students suffering minor illnesses, colds, flu, sore throats, will be stressed by the time lost from school during these illnesses and the depletion of their energies afterwards.

Students attempting to juggle paid work, school and study, often feel under pressure as the year progresses and the demands for study increase. They may be tired and getting insufficient rest. Depleted physical resources are stressful.

Stress and the CAO

What is the CAO?
The method by which a Leaving Cert. student applies for a place in third-level institutes is through the Central Applications Office, known as the CAO.

The declared purpose[1] of the CAO is to provide this central processing of applications for admission to the first year of undergraduate courses in Republic of Ireland institutions. This is a method that was designed to deal with the volume of applications in an efficient and fair manner.

The specific details on how the Central Applications Office system works are contained in the *CAO Handbook,* available from their offices,[2] and parents are advised to read this carefully. Most answers to queries are contained in the handbook, which has both a printed and an online version.[3]

The CAO covers the places in all the colleges including certificate, diploma and degree courses. It also includes the private fee-paying colleges. The advantage of this system is that students can apply for a wide variety of degree and certificate or diploma courses listing their preferences from first choice to tenth choice both on degree courses and on cert./diploma courses.

Some institutions also have particular restrictions, requiring, for example, students to attend an interview or provide a portfolio in addition to their 'points'. These are clearly identified in the handbook. These are called 'Restricted Application Courses'. Their assessments and interviews may occur in March or April of the Leaving Cert. year.

When looking for advice the following is of note:

- All information with regard to CAO is obtainable from the handbook or from the office itself.
- The usual deadline for both paper and online applications is 5.15 p.m. February 1st. The late closing date is 5.15.p.m. on May 1st.
- The CAO provides statements confirming course choices to those applicants who have submitted by February 1st in the Leaving Cert. year.
- There is a change of mind facility usually available up to 1st July. Knowing that this is possible should ease the tension and stress for students.
- After CAO offers have been made some colleges have vacant places. A vacant place arises when a course has been

undersubscribed. These vacant places are usually published in newspapers. Applications for a vacant place should be made through the CAO.

- Parents seeking help in relation to specific queries about colleges should obtain this information directly from the institutes or colleges. For example, information about college fees is obtained from the Fees Offices of the college in which the course is being held.
- The Admissions Office or Accommodation Office of the relevant institute usually provides information about accommodation.

Specific Stresses of Completing CAO Forms

Before online facilities there were many post-office officials who witnessed days of absolute panic by Leaving Cert. students and their parents as the deadline for completion of CAO forms approached. This tended to include checking and rechecking of the contents of the CAO envelopes, the double check that the receipt for fees was enclosed, that the individual items to be included in the application were ticked off on the envelope as these precious contents were entered, sealed and often 'swift-posted' to ensure their safe arrival before the final time for acceptance of applications.

With the introduction of online applications, there is no doubt that similar stresses may be played out in individual homes before family PCs as the deadline approaches.

This anxiety seems to have more to do with the psychological import of completing the forms than with the actual mechanical difficulty of filling in the required information. While there are many people who would see the system as being too narrow, almost exclusively points based[4] and providing no allowance for emotional intelligence and suitability for career choices, the system itself is probably as clear, user-friendly, transparent and comprehensive as it could be.

The stress of the whole CAO process would appear to lie in the enormity of the decision-making in the eyes of students and parents. It is the time when colours must be pinned to the mast, decisions made about what course or institution a student would wish to be in the following year and about the likelihood of achieving that goal.

The following may be helpful to parents and students:

- It is important *not* to make more of this CAO form-filling than necessary. Remember that it is just a form and there is an opportunity for change of mind forms to be entered at a later stage.
- Remember that the irritation that many young people display when asked to complete the form is an expression of their anxiety. It is a time when many students confront psychologically and realistically what they might be able to achieve.
- Some parents find it helpful if they acquaint themselves with the system and read the handbook in advance of discussing the procedure with students. When parents and student sit down to the form together, at least one person understands the process. It is surprising how many students do not actually read the Handbook and, therefore, become stressed by being confronted with a sea of letters and numbers representing colleges and course numbers. If parents are well acquainted with the system they can offer help in this regard to the stressed student.
- Students have always been advised to put their first choice first. It is important that choices are put in order of preference down each list. There have been too many unfortunate instances where a student, doubting their capacity or miscalculating the popularity of a course, missed doing their chosen course because they did not list it first. It would be exceptionally upsetting to find that one had the points for first choice, but had not so listed it.

Parents can help students by reminding them about how the system works. For example, it is important to remember that the points required for courses are primarily based on the demand for places on those courses rather than exclusively on the difficulty level of the courses. Students should *not* evaluate themselves on a points system. There are enough evaluations going on in the Leaving Cert. year without students evaluating themselves negatively based on this system.

Some students are reluctant to commit to several years study required for a degree after the Leaving Cert. These students should consider those colleges that allow annual incremental progress toward a degree. This is done in stages through certificate, diploma and then degree. It is advantageous for the 'uncertain' student to enter a college where they can begin with a certificate. This means that at the end of one year the student has a qualification. If the subject area is of interest and the student is enjoying college life, then that student can continue for a further year to receive a Diploma and finally qualify for an add on Degree.

Parents who think that their child may not be a candidate for the 'long haul' could discuss the Cert./Diploma/Degree option. Life is far more difficult for the student who enters a three or four year degree programme only to discover after a year or two that the area is of no interest.

The range and quality of Post-Leaving Cert. (PLC) courses should not be dismissed. Some of these courses provide training in areas which are not formally credited in other contexts and there are some courses which are regarded as being the highest quality in that area of training.

Parents should remind students that the PLCs also have the practical advantage of being the alternate route to careers the student may not be able to access directly or immediately through CAO. For example some PLC courses lead to places on Certificate courses. Courses in Journalism, Communications and Media Studies are well know for their high standard and for the advantage they may confer on students who subsequently apply through the CAO for places in a third-level college.

Students who are stressed or despondent about the possibility of being able to follow their chosen vocational path might also be reminded of the range of courses in the UK[5] colleges that are available. These applications take into account other information *from* the student and *about* the student from teachers and other relevant referees. Because they are not exclusively points based they can often suit the student who is less able to avail of the Irish points-based system.

Finally, it is important for parents to remind students that there is something for everyone. With the number of colleges, the wealth of available courses, the differing levels of difficulty in courses and the range of areas now being formally accredited in third-level institutes, no student should be without some place that will be rewarding.

Students who are aware of their parent's confidence that there is a rewarding and satisfying career option suited to the student's particular profile of talents will be much less stressed than students who believe that there is only one road to success and that is through high points on coveted places in traditional educational areas.

Previous Losses and Stresses

Students who have suffered stressful events in their lives, are often more vulnerable to any new stressor. The Leaving Cert. threatens 'loss' and any student who has already suffered significant loss, of any kind, may feel this more acutely. This may be the death of a pet, the loss of a friend, losing a girlfriend or boyfriend, parental separation or death of a parent.

The potential losses embedded in the Leaving Cert. are as follows:

- Loss of self-esteem.
- Loss of belief in academic ability.
- Loss of the regard of family and relations.
- Loss of a college place.

Stress of Expectations

Research on stress shows that whether or not something is experienced as stressful often depends on the individual person.

Students with a long and comfortable record of exam success will obviously have far greater confidence than the student repeating the Leaving Cert. or the student for whom exams have always been a struggle. The experience of stress, therefore, depends not only on the event, but also on a person's *perception* of that event and their perception of their ability to cope with it.

What makes a situation particularly stressful is when the demands being made of a person exceed that person's capacity to meet them. The more uncontrollable and threatening a situation seems to be the more stressful it will be.

When students speak about being stressed, what they are often trying to communicate is the gap between what is expected of them and what they believe they can produce. This is when expectations exceed the student's capacity. This can happen to an individual student. It can happen to a group of students in, for example, an A class, or at a wider level.

We know that this can happen at a more national level. For example, many people would regard the number of Leaving Cert. points required for some Third-Level courses to be outside of the scope of many students. Again, the demand for points to enter some professions exceeds most students' capacity to acquire them.

The further twist is that those students who do achieve exceedingly high points then feel compelled to enter those high point courses, regardless of their interest or aptitude in the area. Otherwise the points are 'wasted'.

The stress of this system can weigh upon the student as the exams draw near, reminding the student that 'passing' is not enough, that 'good enough' may not be enough.

Furthermore, students also realise that exams demand that within the space of a few hours they must exhibit their knowledge in subjects on which they have been working for years. Their futures may even depend on it. This is enormous pressure.

Finally, because it is a situation that is inherently stressful for many students they are left with the classic options *fight or flight,* neither of which realistically seem to be available to them. Those students who feel caught in a situation between incapacity to achieve and no possibility of escape will feel the most stress as the year progresses.

Fight or Flight

Stress was originally a survival mechanism for primitive man to protect him from the dangers of his environment. In primitive times this was more likely to be an approaching lion than an approaching exam. Being able to mobilise all physical strength, to fight the animal or to run away at speed was crucial to survival.

But to be on that level of physical alert all the time, is exhausting. Theories of stress emphasise the short-term benefit of an adrenalin rush, but the long-term exhaustion from a state of high alert. What initially motivates us can eventually cause burn-out.

This can happen with regard to study, if periods of rest and relaxation are not built into the timetable. These periods of relaxation, when the body and mind are calm and do not feel under any threat are, therefore, crucial to a student's stress management.

Additionally, prolonged stress can bring about problems in concentration, in memory and in problem solving, all of which are essential to learning. Stress, which depletes the capacity to learn and to remember, will in turn make the student even more stressed, further reducing their learning potential.

As exams approach, the normal escape routes from stress, the famous fight or flight responses seem closed off. The fight, (study) which was a possible way of overcoming the problem at the beginning of 6th year, is less available, as less time is available to study. This is why students worry so much when the exam time draws near.

The flight, (escape) into other distracting activities, social life, TV, alcohol, also becomes increasingly inappropriate. Furthermore, the student can feel overloaded with work. This can either take the form of too much study to do, or study which is too difficult. Both are stressors.

Caught in a situation where the student feels unable to fight or flee, stress increases. This is the time to ensure that the student does not adopt other inappropriate flight forms. Flight into illness is one such example.

However, illness in a student should not automatically be attributed to stress. Sometimes the illness and the exam are purely coincidental. At other times an illness can be heightened by the stress of an exam, or the stress of an exam can be exacerbated by an illness, so that real problems are made worse because the student is physically exhausted.

Furthermore, prolonged stress has an effect on the immune system, weakening a person's defences against illness. It is, therefore, always best to be sure that a medical condition that requires immediate attention is not overlooked, just because it arises as the exam approaches.

Other Forms of Flight
Students may also metaphorically 'take flight' in other ways, which require medical intervention and attention.

- They may take flight in substances. Smoking more, drinking more or drugs.
- They make take flight in sexually promiscuous behaviour.
- They may become acutely anxious.
- They may take risks.
- They may become obsessive about study, being unable to leave the books even for a moment and become distressed at any suggestion that they do so.
- They may develop little rituals, washing excessively, tidying inordinately or becoming over concerned about cleanliness.

- They may become angry, aggressive or oppositional. This is called *externalising* the problem. We should always look behind the external behaviour a young person shows to see what internal psychological distress may be there.[6]
- They may become depressed. This is known as *internalising* the problem. Equally we need to look out for distress that might be hidden when someone is under stress.
- They may be totally unable to cope and disintegrate into withdrawal, secrecy, suspicion or odd behaviour.

Whatever behaviour is produced as a response to stress should be understood from the perspective that adolescent behaviour is usually a *message* from a young person to the adult world.

Often the message is about difficulty, distress or inability to cope. It is important that the message is understood even if it is delivered in an indirect manner.

Messages are sent because there is a need for someone to receive them, interpret them and act upon them.

Panic Attacks

One of the messages that parents need to 'read' is the message sent by a young person who is in a state of panic.

It is also important to understand the difference between what people mean when they say they are panicked and a panic attack or panic disorder.

When students tell each other they are panicking, they are often talking about the uncomfortable feelings of worry about an exam. They are talking about the stress and anxiety they are feeling.

However, when stress and panic is prolonged and there is no way to avoid them, then they can turn into panicky feelings. These feelings of panic can in turn suddenly become a panic attack.

What is a Panic Attack?

A panic attack is a terrifying experience. It is sudden and usually happens without any warning. It is indescribably intense. The body and mind are overwhelmed. There are major physical experiences and monstrous psychological ones in which the person is convinced that they are about to die. It has sometimes been described in terms of a suffocation false alarm; because the body goes into the kind of reaction it would if a person was actually suffocating.

The panic tends to reach and peak and then to subside. But during this time the person suffers the trauma of believing that they are in the grip of a terminal life-threatening event:

- A heart attack.
- A brain tumour.
- Suffocation.
- Choking or strangulation.

Not surprisingly people often end up in casualty in hospital.

Sometimes people think that they have 'lost it' that they are going uncontrollably crazy. This adds to the fear. People who have suffered a panic attack will also talk about

- Feeling extremes of heat or cold.
- They may talk about fear of fainting.
- Sometimes they hear ringing in the ears.
- Sometimes they feel as if they are out of their body looking down at themselves. This adds to the belief that they are dying or even that they have died.
- Because a panic attack can come on when someone is asleep they may wake up in the throes of symptoms, alone, in the dark, imagining they have reached their last and are about to die.

It is important that a student does not have this experience of panic dismissed as a just a fit of exam panic. This would downgrade the student's experience.

Also, it is important to eliminate other medical conditions that have some of the same signs, by getting medical attention as soon as possible.

Finally, students who experience panic attacks will, of course, be terrified of having this experience during the exam. The problem with this fear is that it compounds itself. The outcome of a panic attack is often that the student becomes terrified of having another. The fear leads to what is feared.

Panic disorder requires medical attention. It is not heightened stress; it is of a different physiological and psychological order and one that can incapacitate the student if it is left unattended to. The panic message is one that needs to be heard.

Coping with Stress and Panic

How a student copes with the inevitable stress of the Leaving Cert. exam will depend on many things. These include self-esteem, confidence and psychological hardiness.[7] Research on stress resistant or hardy people shows that they feel in control because of their commitment to work and acceptance of challenges as part of life and as opportunities for growth. It takes a mature and responsible Leaving Cert. student to achieve this.

How a person copes often also depends on the persons' record of coping before in other similar situations. Coping skills are further divided into what are called *problem-focused* coping, which involves trying to change or avoid the situation and *emotion-focused* coping, which attempts to alter emotional reactions to it.

However, receiving emotional support has been found to be particularly effective in coping with stress. This is where parents can play an important role, by providing their children with this vital emotional prop. It is terribly important to have someone 'there', someone who is concerned and caring, and someone in whom the student can confide and trust when they are feeling stressed.

Additionally, the following factors will influence the student's response to stressors:

- Their personal level of maturity, and readiness for this life stage.
- The belief students have in their capacity to succeed in the exam.
- Their actual ability to undertake the academic demands of the exam.
- The support systems that surround them; family, friends and other validating relationships.
- School support. Interest and support of teachers, which is an exceptionally valuable resource.
- How they have coped before in similar situations, and whether that induces confidence or anxiety in the student.
- The degree of threat the thought of failure brings to the student's identity. Those who believe that their worth depends on their accomplishments will obviously be more anxious than students who have other identities.
- Their network of school friends. This support system of comrades in adversity is one of the most important psychological props. It reassures students about the normality of their worries and concerns.
- The physical health of the student.
- The psychological robustness of the student. Whether the student is of an anxious, intense or emotional disposition or alternatively, sturdy, hardy resilient and emotionally strong.
- The extent to which a student ruminates on the problem or actively tries to deal with it. Research shows that ruminating decreases problem solving.
- The degree to which the student has been attending to stress management; walks, exercise, diet, regular sleep, doing relaxation exercises, etc.
- Stress management techniques the student uses; relaxation training, meditation, biofeedback (learning to control physical responses to stress) and cognitive techniques (learning to identify stresses and tackle them).

- Self-esteem. Students whose popularity relies on success will feel under particular stress.
- As noted, the presence of someone to confide in who is sympathetic.
- Belief in capacity to survive regardless of outcome.
- All the other influencing factors that make up the person who is a student.[8]

How Can Parents Help?

While there are differences in people's capacity to cope, here are some additional stress reducers:

Time Management
Students who can be helped to develop a routine and study habits will feel much more in control of the situation than those floundering around without a study pattern. Some of the ideas in Chapter 6 may be useful.

Practise and Rehearse
Turn the dreaded into the familiar because the familiar is rarely dreaded. Familiarity with a feared situation is one of the greatest stress reducers. This is why public speakers often like to view the room in which they will be speaking.

Being able to 'rehearse' and imagine oneself in a situation, reduces the tendency to imagine the worst. Students should therefore, be familiar with the room in which they will be sitting their Mocks and Leaving Cert.

Revision
Similarly students who spend most of the revision time answering Leaving Cert. papers, practising questions, doing timed 'simulated' exams are ensuring that the day of the exam will not be too different from their usual revision sessions.

Expectations
Allied to the above, knowing what is expected in a situation is an important stress reducer. This involves knowing precisely what

the curriculum is, the kind of questions asked, the expected answers and the criteria on which those answers are judged.

Writing Down Worries
It is helpful if students write out their worst fears. At least by putting words on how they feel they can turn worries into problems. Problems can be solved. For example, if worry about the 'Leaving' is really fear of failing Irish, then a grind in Irish might solve some of the worry.

Importance of Sleep
Impress upon students the importance of sleep. Research from Harvard Medical School in 2000 shows that being sleep-deprived can hinder certain types of learning.[9]

Additionally, German research has show that the early stage of a night's sleep sets the brain up to store new information. To improve performance on a new tasks it is important to have a good sleep the first night after learning it.

Harnessing Stress
Adopting a lifestyle that recognises the importance of harnessing the motivating aspects of stress and controlling the distressing aspects, is one of the important lessons of the Leaving Cert. year and a life-long skill for those who can acquire it.

More Points for Parents

Listen to their Worries
The well-intentioned parent may tell a student who complains about a school subject, 'don't worry, you'll be fine'. That is not what the student wants to hear. A student who thinks all will be fine in a subject does not have a need to raise the matter with parents. The student is trying to open up a discussion about their worries. Saying, 'you'll be fine', closes the conversation.

Praise and Encourage their Efforts

It has been shown that praise is a more potent motivator for young people than being given 'objects' as rewards. Criticism is exceptionally damaging to young people.

Protect them from Work Overload

It is difficult for students if they have to work excessively outside home for money or at home in a way that would disrupt their studies. The fatigue from work, from school and from study can become too much for them to cope with.

If possible, it is advised that students give up paid work in the weeks before their exams and during the exams.

Give Optimistic Reminders

It is also very useful if parents provide reminders that the stress is time-limited and will soon be over. Remarks such as *'you'll be glad when this is over and you can relax'* or *'imagine, it will all be over soon'* help students to see that difficult situations come to an end.

This is another important life lesson that the Leaving Cert. can provide, an opportunity to weather a normal life storm, have the confidence that one can survive and know that it is a matter of hanging in there in the interim.

Conversation Openers

In addition to emphasising that stress is a fact of life and is usually time-limited, parents can also help students to talk during those times that are stressful.

While students sometimes do not want to talk about their worries, it is helpful if parents let the student know that they are available any time the student *would* like to do so. Additionally, parents usually observe their children and can identify the opportunities to open up discussions in which students may then be able to express their worries and fears.

Conversation openers to students can be given, such as *'you must be tired'* or *'I'm sure you're feeling a bit fed-up'*. Or *'this is a difficult time for you, isn't it?* This is helpful because sometimes students *do* want to talk about how they feel, but do not know where to begin. Suggesting that worry is normal can be a way to help them talk.

Parents who notice their student looking down can remark on it casually. For example, it can open a conversation to say *'You're looking a bit glum?'* or *'Do you think it will never end?'*

Sometimes a parent can remind a student that they understand what they are going through by saying something like. 'I can't remember which is worse the pressure or the study?'

Students really appreciate if a parent acknowledges that things are more difficult and more stressful now with the points system than they were in their parents' time.

Some possible remarks include:

It's so much harder on you than in my time. We just had to pass.
It's the competition that makes it so difficult isn't it?
We were lucky; none of us would have got into third-level if we had
*   to get all those points.*
Do you think the exam is unfair?
What's your biggest worry about the Leaving?
If you had a magic wand now, what would you wish for?
Do you think you can hang on in there until it is all over?

Feeling that their stress is understood is exceptionally helpful for young people. Additionally, understanding that normal living often includes stressful and non-stressful periods is important.

Students who learn for the future that one must meet the challenge of difficult times and enjoy the reprieve of pleasant times will be equipped to deal with some of the vicissitudes of life.

No False Reassurances

Parents often get anxious when their child speaks about stress and worry. Because of this they sometimes jump in with false reassurance without realising that in so doing they may be dismissing an important request for help.

It may relieve parents' anxiety to end the discussion but it sends the student away unheard. Parents never intend to do this. It is because of their love and concern for their children that it is hard for parents to hear that they are unhappy or anxious.

It is helpful, instead, if parents can ask the student to tell them about the anxiety. Questions such as the following are suggested:

What does that feel like?
When do you feel it?
Is it there all the time?
When did it start? Is it getting worse?
Can you sleep with it? Does it wake you up?
Is it making you fed up? Is it making you feel afraid?
Is it stopping you from studying? Is it making it hard to concentrate?
Does it make you tired?
Are there times when it is very bad? Are there times when it is not too bad?
I'm sorry you are worried; can I help in any way?
I'm so glad you told me. I would want to know what's happening with you and I would want to help.
What do you think would help you with it?
Is there anything you would like me to do?

These questions[10] are not an interrogation, but questions to be asked slowly and gently. Seeking a full description is crucial. Firstly, it allows the parent to judge how serious the anxiety is and whether or not it might need professional attention. Secondly, it shows respect for the young person's feelings. Thirdly, it shows how interested the parent is in genuinely knowing what is going on for their son or daughter.

Finally, it demonstrates to the young person that talking about feelings will get a positive response.

Notes

1   *CAO Handbook.*
2   Toner House, Eglinton Street, Galway
    Tel 091-509800.
    Mon-Fri 9.30am-1.00pm and 2.00pm-5.15pm
3   www.cao.ie
4   See Chapter 1 for discussion of this.
5   Information through UCAS University and College Admissions Service, Fulton House, Jessop Avenue, Cheltenham, Gloucestershire, GLE 50 335H, England.
6   See Chapter 10 on depression for further discussion of this.
7   Kobasa, S.C. (1979) 'Stressful Life Events, personality and health: an inquiry into hardiness', *Journal of Personality and Social Psychology* 37, 1-11.
8   Outline in Chapter 2.
9   Cited earlier. See Chapter 6.
10 These are also useful questions if you think your child may be depressed. See Chapter 10 on depression.

9

THE LEAVING CERT. IN DIFFICULT CIRCUMSTANCES

There are many situations that make the Leaving Cert. a more difficult process for some students than for others. While these are too numerous to deal with in any depth, some circumstances that add to the normal pressures of 6th year are considered below:

- Being a repeat student, which makes the second attempt at the Leaving Cert. far more significant because of the different psychological anxieties it imposes.
- Suffering chronic illness. A student struggling with asthma, diabetes, epilepsy, chronic fatigue, acute anxiety or depression or indeed any medical complaint that adds to the normal pressures of 6th year or which may require special conditions when sitting the exam.
- Having a specific learning disability such as dyslexia or dysgraphia, or any of the other 'written language disorder' elements, which may require a different approach to learning. There are additional stresses imposed by these disabilities both in day-to-day school life and in the Leaving Cert. exam situation where special consideration may be required.
- Being gifted. Being different almost always causes difficulties at school. Giftedness often has its own unrecognised problems.
- Educational disadvantage. This can take many forms, being either a relative condition or a condition of objective hardship, which places stress on the student.

- Difficult family circumstances and the strains they can impose on the student at the adolescent life stage during Leaving Cert. year.
- Specific family circumstances, such as the death of a parent or parental separation during the school year and the concomitant grief and mourning at what is already a difficult time in adolescence.

Repeating The Leaving Cert.

Students who repeat the Leaving Cert. often feel exceptionally stressed. While it might appear that repeating would carry the benefit of having been through the process before, it also puts greater pressure on the student to succeed. This needs to be acknowledged and addressed. Otherwise the fears that may build up in the student can bring about the unthinkable situation of having a problem with the Leaving Cert. for a second time.

The reasons why a student has to repeat will, of course, play a part in how the student and others perceive their having to repeat in the first place. If the reason was beyond the student's control, for example a road traffic accident, then the student will feel much less stressed than if the repeat is because of poor results on the previous attempt. Obviously the views of parents and friends will also play a big part in how the repeat student views the situation.

Reasons for Repeating
A student may have to repeat for the following reasons:

- Suffering an accident, injury or illness during the Leaving Cert. exams and having to sit the entire exam again.
- Becoming stressed out, suffering a panic attack or finding oneself mentally unable to continue.
- Serious illness or death in a family member during the exam.
- Family situations such as parental separation and divorce that brought the exams to abrupt closure.

- Achieving well, but receiving insufficient points to pursue a chosen third level course or job. Some courses have such high requirements that despite good Leaving Cert. results the points required are insufficient to enter that particular college.

Concerns of Repeat Students
Students who are repeating need particular support. The following are their expressed concerns:

- Repeat students feel much more threatened than first time Leaving Cert. students because their self-esteem and academic esteem may be at stake.
- Repeating also puts them out of synchrony with their peers. Suddenly, their classmates have moved on to jobs or college or courses while the repeat student is still a schoolboy or schoolgirl.
- There is an enormous psychological gap between having left school and still being in a school uniform, so to speak. This makes it difficult for repeat students to retain the perspective that within about ten months they will have 'caught up' again.
- Similarly, it can be hard to go out with last-years' school friends at the weekend who are now talking about 'Fresher's Week' or their new friends on a course when the repeat student is still trudging their weary way to school.
- Many repeat students express distress at placing an additional financial burden on parents, particularly if private education has to be provided to repeat.
- Some students feel that expectations for success will be exceptionally high, given that the student has already been through the exam system.
- Alternatively, people can think that the student is not stressed at all because they have been through the exam before. The opposite is often the case.
- Others say that they are afraid of disappointing or embarrassing their parents if after a second trial they do not increase their 'points'.

- Some students find that they are bored early in the year by the repeat of material that carries no novelty. This can be de-motivating and a disincentive to study.
- Other students say that they are disadvantaged because some of the prescribed material has changed. For example, they have to 'forget' the prescribed Shakespearian play from the previous year and take on an entirely new play. This can be confusing.
- Finally, in instances where an accident, illness or the death of a parent caused the student to have to repeat, memories of the trauma and upset can be re-evoked as the Leaving Cert. approaches causing anniversary anxiety and distress.

What Can a Parent Do?
There are some things a parent can do which are very reassuring to the repeat student. Here are suggestions.

- It is particularly important to let the repeat student know that you are aware of the extra stress of being a repeat student.
- Reassure the student that expectations are not unrealistic because the student is repeating. Explain that you are aware that there can even be disadvantages to that. You could cite the example given above, of having to tackle some new material in one year on which current students have already spend a year.
- It is particularly important that parents acknowledge the difficulties that can arise for the student when going out with their old friends who have 'moved on'. However, it is important that the repeat student does not try to lead a similar social life to the friends in third-level or in employment. Their situation is different and their study routine and pace of lifestyle is different to that of the Leaving Cert. student.
- Ask the student to identify, from their experience of last year, what supports you provided that were helpful and if there are additional supports that would have assisted.

- The way that a parents reassure a repeat student will, of course, depend on why the student had to repeat the Leaving Cert. in the first place. For example, if it was a family bereavement, the parent will want to remind the student that it is normal to be upset when thinking of 'this time last year'. If it was an accident, reassure the student that the chance of another accident is highly unlikely. If the student was mentally unable to do the exam, talk about how grateful you are that they are now feeling better and *that* is what is most important.
- Whatever the circumstances, reassurance is required. Even if your child did not study at all last year and that is why it is necessary to repeat the Leaving Cert. this year, your child has either learned from this experience and will study better this year, or has still not grown up enough to be able to do so. In this case admonishments will have as little effect this year as they had last year. What will be effective is if you lay down friendly, but firm, boundaries about study and social life to ensure that this repeat year does not get frittered away.

Suffering Chronic Illness

Students who suffer from a chronic medical condition are often mature and resilient in coping with their difficulty.

Students suffering from epilepsy, students with diabetes, students with asthma, students suffering from chronic fatigue or students with a significant visual impairment who have coped through secondary school, have clearly adjusted to the demands, self-monitoring, intervention and self-care required by the condition.

Having said that, many illnesses are exacerbated by stress and the stresses inherent in sitting the Leaving Cert. can shift a chronic illness into an acute episode, which obviously requires attention.

Special Arrangements for the Leaving Cert.

Parents may wish to know that the Department of Education and Science[1] offers students in these circumstances special arrangements to sit the exams in a separate room.

For example, a student with asthma may require the use of a nebulizer during exams, a student with dyslexia may need to use a word-processor, and a student who breaks a limb and is in hospital can nonetheless be facilitated to take the exam from their hospital bed.

Additionally, a student who is a visually challenged can receive enlarged papers or papers in Braille.

These special arrangements offered by the Department of Education and Science, are called 'Reasonable Accommodation' and apply to those with either physical disabilities or specific learning disabilities that require special exam arrangements.

What Can a Parent Do?
Students may feel different because of special arrangements and most adolescents do not welcome being different to peers.

- It is helpful if parents acknowledge to students that they may feel a little different at the outset because of the special arrangements.
- Also understand that students sometimes feel they will miss out on gauging the reaction of peers to the exam papers when they are handed out, noting the speed of writing of classmates or simply being in the exam hall milieu.
- Reassure the student that these feelings will soon wear off.
- Remind the student that there are also the advantages of no distractions from others, shuffling, sighing, coughing, seeking the attention of the invigilator, dropping pens or leaving the exam room.
- Finally, the student who sits the exam in a separate room in the school can nonetheless join peers before and after the exam for the pre-exam psyche up and the post-exam 'autopsy'.

All schools are issued with advice packs on this procedure so parents can ask about this in the student's school, through whom the arrangements are made. Alternatively advice can be received directly from the Department of Education and Science.

Specific Learning Difficulties

The area of 'specific learning difficulties' is a vast and complex area. It would require an entire book to even begin to explore the many manifestations, not to mention the academic implications of having a specific leaning difficulty, or SLD, and particularly the significance of this for the Leaving Cert. student.[2]

SLD is one of the terms to cover the variety of presentations of dyslexia, which itself is probably more properly termed a Written Language Disorder (WLD).

Could my Leaving Cert. Student be Dyslexic?
Believe it or not, it is possible for a person to go through the entire school system with what has been called a 'hidden dyslexia'. That is, with a number of the less obvious symptoms, because of the complexity of the combination of symptoms, or because the person has used their good general intelligence to hide or circumvent the problem.

The statistics of the number of people registered as being dyslexic at second level is well below the estimated incidence of the difficulty in a population. It is not uncommon for a secondary school teacher to query dyslexia in a student and have their opinion confirmed by subsequent assessment. This can occur even in 6th year.

For that reason it may be useful to point out some of the aspects of the disorder to look out for.

- Dyslexia is a disorder in which individuals process written information differently. There are often the obvious problems in reading, and small words are particularly confusing. Sometimes there are problems in seeing the difference between letters of similar appearance such as 'p' 'q' or 'd' and 'b'. There may be difficulties in spelling, in expressing ideas in written form and in writing legibly.

- In addition to the obvious reading, writing and spelling problems, dyslexia may involve problems in one or more of the following: understanding the written word, composing sentences which are intelligible, punctuating them, knowing when to use capitals and when to use lower case or smaller letters. In summary any communication that goes from the page to the brain or from the brain to the page.
- To explain further, written language information is transported from *page to brain* when we read. It goes from *brain to page* when we write. To carry out these tasks we also have to have a proficiency in other aspects of language, these can include speaking, word-finding and expressing ideas, understanding what people are saying, following instructions and directions, being able to sequence ideas, follow a story line, tell a coherent story, carry out instructions and follow directions by forming a mental map.
- There are early signs a child may be dyslexic that parents may remember, one of the most prevalent being *not crawling as a baby*. There is often early speech and language hesitancy or delay.
- There can be problems in telling right from left. More left-handed than right-handed people have dyslexia and even if the person with dyslexia is not left-handed there is usually left-handedness somewhere in the family, grandfather, aunt or uncle.
- There can be problems in judging the passage of time and being confused about dates and times. Homework and information may get copied incorrectly from the blackboard and the student who is 'brilliant' in some subjects may always have disappointing written exam results.
- There may be a love of things mechanical and technological, of computers and graphics, of interior design, of film and all things visual and intricate.

- There may be a hatred of language-based subjects, or at least hatred when they are assessed in a timed, written exam.
- People may describe the student as 'in one ear and out the other' and the student may be misconstrued as careless or lazy especially because there may be poor presentation of homework and disorganisation beyond the patience of the most placid of teachers and parents!

Indeed, some of the problems being described here will remind parents of the problems of the disorganised, time-mismanaging student described in Chapter 6.

Causes of Dyslexia
Dyslexia tends to run in families, suggesting that there is a genetic basis.[3] Research using modern brain scans of people reading (FMRI)[4] shows that people with this condition tend to process information in the brain differently. In fact instead of a disorder, we should probably talk about a *Learning Difference.*[5]

More boys than girls have dyslexia, in a ratio of about four to one. Some would suggest an even higher ratio because of the natural propensity to precocity in language by girls. This is often observed in the greater maturity in development of the language areas in their brains and the communication between parts of the brain. Indeed, one of the descriptions from the Yale research about the way the brain of a person with dyslexia operates is that there is 'a glitch in the wiring'.

Having said that, those who have worked with people who have dyslexia will know that the same 'glitch' often produces high levels of creativity and intellect. It is as if the light that will not go on in one circuit of the brain lights up even more brightly in another area. Indeed, Edison, inventor of the light bulb, lit up the world for the rest of us out of his own dyslexic circuitry.

The international figures for dyslexia put severe incapacitating dyslexia at 2 per cent but variants of as high as 10 per cent[6] are suggested and it is dreadfully under diagnosed.

If approximately sixty thousand students sit the Leaving Cert., then as many as six thousand could conceivably have some variant of the problem. It is worth looking out for it if your student has had their struggles with language and written language over the years at school.

What Should a Parent Do?
If you think that your child may have a difficulty it is important to get this identified as quickly as possible to avail of the arrangements provided by the Department of Education and Science.

- Get a psychoeducational assessment by a psychologist.[7] Remember, the distinguishing factor in dyslexia is that there is marked under-achievement in most aspects of language including written language. This is in comparison with good overall intellectual ability, at least average and often above average.
- Parents may also wish to consult with The Psychological Society of Ireland, PSI[8] which retains a list of qualified registered psychologists.
- Parents are also advised to consult with a Speech and Language Therapist who is specialist in this area. This assessment is central to the diagnostic and treatment process. Speech and Language Therapists can often pinpoint the *precise* language-processing areas that are causing the problem and their approach to helping students can bring about significant improvements.
- Parents could also contact the Association for Children and Adults with Learning Difficulties (ACLD).[9] They can assist with assessment, diagnosis, intervention and support.
- If you child does have dyslexia, then immediate application for special arrangements in the Leaving Cert. examination may need to be made through the school to the Department of Education and Science accompanied by a psychological report, samples of the student's schoolwork and the opinion of the student's teachers. However, the usual requirement is that such applications be made in the year prior to the year

in which a student sits the exam, usually about eighteen months before the Leaving Cert. exam.

- Special arrangements for the exam may also include someone to read the exam paper to the student. Application can be made for word-processing, Dictaphone, tape-recorder or other mechanical aids for the student who is unable to write. A scribe or amanuensis may be required. In some instances a person expert in deciphering the writings of people with dyslexia is assigned to the evaluation of the student's paper. Indeed, all examiners are instructed to refer any indecipherable scripts by *any* student to the advising examiner.
- Allowance or a *waiver* may also be made with regard to spelling and grammatical elements, but the actual results of the Leaving Cert. may have this recorded on an accompanying explanatory note with their certificate.
- Sometimes an exemption from studying Irish is given to students who have such severe dyslexia that they have *'failed to cope with a first language or "mother tongue"'*. Again substantial assessment evidence is obviously required for this.
- Finally, parents need to remind their student who has dyslexia of the many brilliant architects, engineers, mechanics, artists, surgeons, craftsmen, inventors, scientists, presidents, sculptors and visionaries from the ranks of those who learn in this different way. Amongst the most famous would probably be Einstein and Leonardo da Vinci.

People with this learning difference require all the support that the educational system can provide and the Department of Education and Science has recognised some of their needs by providing psychological assessment[10] to identify the problem and to provide exemption and examination arrangements to accommodate some of the difficulties that arise for students.

Being Gifted

One may wonder how being gifted could possibly fall into the category of difficulties. There are many reasons why this may be.

Most theories of intelligence look at how a person adapts to the world. But there are many instances in which the world needs to adapt to the child. This is evident in the last section about Specific Learning Disabilities, where the manner in which a person learns or conveys what they know is different. It requires different methods of input and different methods of output. If only one (such as the current almost exclusive written, timed examination) were allowed the person would be gagged from exhibiting their knowledge or worth at all.

People who have different intellectual capacities across the range of multiple intelligences often learn differently. It is not just that they may learn content more quickly; it is a qualitatively different approach to learning and to the world that is dissonant with much of the required regular classroom activity, particularly in an examination year.

Gifted people, in the formally assessed meaning of that word (using the range of criteria that currently are used to determine giftedness), therefore, learn differently, just like the person with Specific Learning Difficulties. Indeed, many people who are gifted are also to be found among those with SLD. This is a double whammy of being gifted and having an SLD that makes a young person feel that they do not fit anywhere at all into the normal scheme of things. Surprisingly to some, they have a higher incidence of left-handedness and as noted an allied higher incidence of Specific Learning Difficulties. Writing skill is often affected and it is not unusual for a 'gifted child' to be unable to write legibly for many years. Einstein, with his reported difficulty with reading and writing, his problems gaining access to college, and his lifelong dyslexia, is the oft-quoted example.

But it is the story that also proves the rule. Many of those who have exceptional talent have gone through early childhood being variously described as 'difficult', 'hyperactive', 'slow', 'disruptive' or 'remedial' with 'careless writing' and 'poor homework'. In short misunderstood, misconstrued and miserable.

Additionally, people who are defined as gifted also often exhibit what has been termed 'overexcitabilities', with typical excessive energy in every area. The abilities of the person are excited by ideas, by learning, by strong emotions, by compassion, by notions of injustice, by quest for knowledge, for content, for input, for rationale for everything. This may also include interest in problem-solving, in abstraction, reflection, analysis, theory and even the philosophical ideas behind the school course content. It may encompass capacity for rich and intense emotions that are difficult to contain, energy that has no outlet and reduced sleep requirement. It is 'seeing reality in a different, stronger and more multisided manner'.[11]

Furthermore, the length of time it often takes to identify that a child is gifted can render the student more vulnerable in traditional academic contexts. Besides, the combination of high intellectual capacity and poor ability to demonstrate that intelligence in traditional forms is often a source of extreme frustration.

The problems for the gifted Leaving Cert. student may therefore be as follows:

- Struggling with negative attitudes toward the school system in a way that may thwart progress in the system. This is unfortunate as Leaving Cert. is obviously a necessary step to many of the learning contexts that could excite the student in the future. Besides, most third-level colleges have excellent understanding and facilities for those with SLDs and those who learn differently.
- Being bored by the repetitive nature of the curriculum or by the restricted manner in which information is being discussed.
- Having a vocabulary that is different to and even inaccessible to peers in a way that is alienating for them or that excludes the student who is gifted.

- People holding an (erroneous) belief, that because a student is gifted that they do not have to work at all, that somehow the information will manifest itself in the brain without any teaching or learning.
- This can create unrealistic expectations of success. The idea that if a person is gifted this will automatically produce eight A1s.
- Having giftedness in one subject, but struggling in another. Giftedness is often highly specific. It may be confined to languages or confined to logical mathematical areas. It is not across the board in all instances. This can expose the student to the dual difficulties of being utterly bored in one class and struggling greatly in another.
- Being supersensitive to the emotional tone in the class, to any observations of callousness by other students towards each other, to the personal experience of this, being the butt of jokes or being excluded.
- Having ideas, aspirations, and excitement about subjects that are not shared by peers. Feeling alone in the world.
- Suffering from perfectionism so that the student is never satisfied by any piece of work completed. Indeed, completing work can be a specific problem as the student strives for excellence rather than just getting the work done.
- Even when work is completed there is often a tendency to be unhappy with it. The Leaving Cert. year poses a particular challenge to the person who is gifted to do 'enough' to do what is required and to complete assignments on time.
- Having problems in exam situations. Being unable to confine ideas to the question asked and knowing when that question has been answered. Too many tangents can mean that the examiner is left with a suffusion of unconnected, self-contained ideas that bear little relation to the simple question asked.
- Suffering from other vulnerabilities, emotionally or socially, that are not recognised or that are dismissed to being gifted.

It is impossible in the context of this chapter to profile the many manifestations of giftedness. The above provides a small sample of the more obvious problems that arise in the educational context. What is important is to remember that those who have different ways of learning require the same supports as each other and that they all require support, particularly in this stressful Leaving Cert. year.

Educational Disadvantage

As the Leaving Cert. becomes more competitive, disadvantage can take relative forms. In other words, there are students to whom so much help and material advantage is given that other students cannot compete.

Some students receive additional grinds, travel abroad, have expensive technological assistance, personal transport, assistance with homework, stress-management and time-management courses. They may have all the videotapes, audiotapes, summary notes, revision books, filofaxes or electronic organisers at their disposal. Every conceivable aid may be provided to the student.

It is important that this does not dishearten other students or parents who cannot afford these advantages. After all, the student who has to self-motivate, to stick with a problem until it is solved, who has to learn to organise his or her own time and who has to achieve on the basis of their own work, has a wealth of other advantages from the experience of the Leaving Cert. year that cannot be bought.

Having said that, there are some students who clearly operate under greater difficulty than others. Research shows the many dimensions under which one can be educationally disadvantaged. Practical disadvantages can occur in poor or overcrowded housing with students having to battle for a place or space in which to study. In these situations, some have to cope with excessive noise or the intrusive sounds of television, neighbours or the surrounding neighbourhood.

Family need for money may require the young person to work excessively to provide for basic educational needs, books, bus fare and sustenance. There are also some young people who feel obliged to leave school to take up paid employment in order to assist family finances.

Additionally, there are those who are disadvantaged by the type of educational facilities available to them, which can vary from one geographical location to the next. Deficits or difficulties in accessing the following can also cause disadvantage:

- Distance from a suitable school.
- School building, room size, sound proofing.
- Laboratories for science, language and computer studies.
- Canteen and catering facilities.
- Sports and recreation opportunities.
- Class composition and class size.
- Pupil-teacher ratio.
- Availability of learning support teachers.
- Support of home-school liaison officers.
- Presence of guidance counsellors.
- Pastoral care service.
- School psychological services and appropriate local adolescent mental health centres.
- Access to psychoeducational assessment and services.

Despite all efforts to equalise opportunities for students, there are some students who *do* have more educational opportunity and support than others. This needs, at least, to be acknowledged to the student who is disadvantaged. Recognition often brings validation. It is important that students who are disadvantaged in any way know that people are aware of the additional stresses on them.

If you, as a parent, believe your child has suffered any educational disadvantages then it is important that your child knows that you are aware of this and the extent to which you admire the student for trying hard, even against the odds.

Family Circumstances

In addition to educational disadvantage, some young people have to cope with enormously difficult family situations. Indeed, there are many young people who, at this crucial educational stage, may encounter family situations that directly affect their health, happiness, mental health or capacity to undertake the requirements of an examination.

Family situations that can place great additional stress on students, and which often require medical, psychiatric or social service intervention include the following:

- Alcoholism in a parent. In a situation where a parent is suffering from alcoholism, this can bring enormous stress to the spouse/partner and children in the family. Tension, intimidation, fearfulness, unpredictability of parental mood, experiences of maudlin approach or hurtful rejection, of being ridiculed or of witnessing parental grandiosity can occur. Additionally, the young person may be blamed for the parent's drinking problem or may feel responsible. There may also be financial hardship arising from the expense of the alcohol or indiscreet decisions made under the influence of alcohol. These are but some of the consequences of this situation that can be suffered by family members. While the person suffering from alcoholism may refuse help, other family members can benefit by family therapy and assistance in coping with the stress of living in such a household.

- Serious psychiatric illness. This may be a situation where one parent has a psychiatric disorder and the other parent is witnessing the extent to which this is stressing the children in the family. Sometimes a brother or sister of the Leaving Cert. student may be suffering a medical or a psychiatric disorder that is taking the entire parental attention away from the Leaving Cert. student and on to the ill sibling. This can silence the student from seeking any assistance knowing that parents are already overburdened.

- Family violence. There are instances where a young person may have to witness violence in the home from one parent to the other. This can cause permanent fear and intimidation, chronic stress in anticipation of the next outburst or event, minor to more serious physical injury if the young person intervenes to protect the other parent or younger brothers and sisters.

- Chronic illness or disability in a family member that requires extensive assistance by the student. Sometimes, there is a parent who requires physical help because of a disability. For example, where the assistance of a son or daughter is required to help lift a disabled parent in and out of a wheelchair.

- Care taking. Sometimes the student is required to help by looking after younger brothers and sisters, preparing meals, and contributing significantly to household tasks. The degree to which the family may come to rely on the assistance of a student may impose enormous strain and cut the young person off from the usual supports of this age and stage, in particular meeting friends and having a normal social life.

- Financial crises. A family may go through a financial crisis and have to sell the family home. A student may have to finance him or herself almost entirely. At this stage, young people are acutely conscious of money and aware of the difficulties that lack of money brings. Having to spend long hours in paid employment is not conducive to study and normal Leaving Cert. student life.

- Sometimes an ill grandparent may move into the student's home during an examination year. The student may be torn between affection for a grandparent and the stress of studying for exams. The family home may become more crowded with another member. Parents may become more stressed caring for another family member. The student may be woken at night if the elderly person is ill or in need of assistance. There may be a wish to spend time with the grandparent, but a consciousness of the limitations of time, particularly as exams approach.

What Should a Parent Do?

There are many difficult life situations that can befall a family at seminal educational times. The Leaving Cert. is no different. What is important, however, is that the difficulty is acknowledged to the student, that the school is made aware of the problem and that appropriate support is sought from the many services available to help individuals and families in difficult situations.

Sometimes this means that all the family may attend family therapy[12] to examine the impact of the difficulty on each family member.

Sometimes a young person is also referred to a health service for additional individual support, to have an adult from outside the family to talk to and confide in.

In some instances adolescents get linked in to support groups with other young people of a similar age who are experiencing the same kind of problems. This can be exceptionally supportive. It helps to meet and compare notes with other young people encountering the same adverse conditions.

It also reduces a young person's sense of isolation, shame and uniqueness in a difficult situation.

Talking to the School

It is helpful if teachers are made aware if there are difficult family circumstances, so that special allowance can be made for the student who is late to school, who may have problems providing homework assignments or who may even be reacting irritably or emotionally in class. This is essential to ensure that the student under pressure at home does not also experience pressure at school because teachers have not been informed.

Clearly a student operating in any of the above circumstances is in a stressful situation and one that requires the understanding, assistance and support of as many adults as possible. A sympathetic interest or a favourable comment can go a long way with an adolescent whose self-esteem has been diminished by family problems.

Any parent who is worried that their Leaving Cert. adolescent is in a difficult family situation should seek professional help initially through their GP, or Health Board or Health Authority after which appropriate referral can be made to the more specialist services in the area which deal with whatever the family situation is.

Death of a Parent or Parental Separation

Tragic family circumstance can occur at any time and sometimes coincide with an exam year. How these situations are managed will depend on the student's mental health and capacity to continue studying for the Leaving Cert. and to sit the exam.

Losses that have particular impact on adolescents in their Leaving Cert. year are the following:

- Death of a parent.
- Parental separation and divorce.

Death of a parent usually evokes distress, mourning and grief. So, too, in a different way, does parental separation, which signals the death of previous family life and which also usually involves the absence of one parent from the family home.

Grief is a very personal response and how a person responds in the face of death of a parent or parental separation is determined by a multitude of factors. These include:

- The relationship with the parent or family member who dies or who leaves home.
- The degree to which the adolescent was prepared for the loss or was taken by surprise.
- The extended family support systems.

- Previous experiences of loss.
- The personal resilience and coping capacity of the young person.
- The resilience of other family members, particularly the surviving parent.

From the point of view of the Leaving Cert. much will depend on how close to exams the death or departure occurs. In both situations of loss most parents would wish that the life of the adolescent would not be further affected by missing the opportunity to move along with the peer group and sit the forthcoming exam.

When the loss is through death, the remaining parent is sometimes concerned that it might seem very callous or disrespectful to the person who died for the adolescent to sit the exam. However, if the adolescent feels able for it, sitting the exam at the expected time can have therapeutic benefit provided there are no unrealistic expectations of a grieving student.

Some young people who have sat their exams in such circumstances have said later that they were able to postpone their grief while focusing on their exam and that this was valuable. It provided a sense of control at a time of loss, it reassured the surviving parent and it made the adolescent feel normal during an abnormal time. It also meant that the grief could be entered into totally when the summer arrived, allowing time for the full flow of grief and loss in a particularly therapeutic way.

Parental separation can be particularly difficult because an adolescent may hide it from friends, classmates and teachers. It does not carry the public recognition and sympathy for the student that losing a parent through death provides, although the adolescent may experience it in a similar way.

In instances of parental separation, it is important that young people do not have their normal activities further disrupted and that the student is not deprived of sitting the Leaving Cert. exam if he or she feels able to do so. Otherwise, the sense of difference from peers can be even more extended and can cause resentment later towards parents for the timing of the separation.

Furthermore, being unable to sit the Leaving Cert. exam because of parental separation can exacerbate an already tense family situation.

Obviously each family must decide what is right for their particular Leaving Cert. student in difficult family circumstances.

What Should a Parent Do?

In making such decisions parents who wish to help their Leaving Cert. student may find the following points useful:

- Make contact with the school to ensure teachers are fully informed of the event and the impact on the student.
- Seek the advice of teachers about the degree to which the student is academically able to continue in the circumstance.
- Remember that grief and loss have significant impact on a student's capacity to concentrate, to commit material to memory and to recall what has been learnt. Distractibility is common as thoughts race about the new situation. This means that loss early in the Leaving Cert. year can cause real academic disadvantage.
- Be vigilant for anxiety and depression and seek help if necessary. Remember that irritability, sleeplessness or alternatively staying in bed all morning, difficult or disruptive behaviour or indulgence in alcohol or drugs can also be signs of depression.
- While offering the young person the choice of sitting the exam or not, it is important to try to remove academic stress or high expectations from the young person.
- Some parents, depending on the vulnerability of the student, suggest postponement of the exams. This is often suggested if the loss occurs within weeks of the exam.
- Alternatively, some parents encourage the young person to sit the exam, but reframe the Leaving Cert. as a trial run, or a rehearsal, without major expectations of achievement.

Knowing that expectations to achieve are removed can often result in students doing much better than expected and carry the added advantage that students usually feel a sense of accomplishment at having been able to sit the exam at the expected time with their peers.

- Finally, be prepared for reactions after the exam. Sometimes young people can keep going bravely until the exam ends after which they may be flooded and overwhelmed with the full impact of their loss. It is important that it is understood that this is normal and that it is prepared for.

Conclusion

Students battling against the odds, in whatever form that may take, deserve all the support and encouragement that the adult world can provide.

Whether it is the pressure of repeating the Leaving, the stress of life events, the tragedy of bereavement, the disadvantage of a dissonant learning style or suffering personal illness, injury or incapacity; whatever the problem adult affirmation and support is required.

Young people need to know that life's problems are containable or solvable, that they can be lived with, adjusted to and survived. The student operating under difficult circumstances has a unique opportunity to learn that lesson.

The parent of that student has a special chance to show that it is not the problems we encounter in life, but how we deal with them, that determine who we are.

This is one of the most important life qualifications we can achieve.

Notes

1 Department of Education and Science, Special Arrangements Policy Section, Exam's Branch, Cornamaddy, Athlone. Telephone 00 353 902 74621.

2 The Department of Education and Science points out that the term 'Specific Learning Disability' does not include disabilities due to poor general intellectual functioning or problems arising from poor attendance at school, poor motivation or other social problems.

3 British researchers have reported finding three common genes associated with dyslexia in blood samples of people with dyslexia and their families. Twin studies also suggest a genetic basis.

4 Research in Yale University (Shaywitz et al, 1998) using magnetic resonance imaging (FMRI) with people with dyslexia, recorded a pattern of under-activation in a large area at the back of the brain associated with language. This shows the neurobiological nature of their reading difficulty.

5 I would propose DLS as the term to signify a Different Learning Style.

6 Dr Beve Hornsby 1984 (See Refs).

7 Department of Education and Science, National Educational Psychological Service Agency. For psychological service to primary and post primary schools, Frederick Court, 24/27 North Frederick Street Dublin. Telephone 00 353 1 8892700.

8 Psychological Society of Ireland, 2a, Corn Exchange Place, Dublin 2. Telephone 00 353 1 6717122.

9 ACLD or Dyslexia Association of Ireland, 1 Suffolk Street, Dublin 2. Telephone 00 353 1 6790276.

10 However, many complain that waiting lists are excessively long.

11 Dabrowski, K. (1972), *Psychoneurosis is not an illness*, Gryf, London.

12 Healy, N. and Murray, M. (2002) 'The Role of Family Therapy in Psychiatry', *Irish Psychiatrist* 3.3 April/May 2002

10

DEPRESSION IN THE LEAVING CERT. STUDENT

Few Leaving Cert. students agree that 'school days are the happiest days of your life'. They remind adults that they are the only people who believe this incredible cliché, that life for the current Leaving Cert. student is a competitive challenge that leaves limited time for this mythical, nostalgic, unspecified 'happiness'. They object to the implication that they are having the best of times, when the reality for many is that they are experiencing the worst of times.

Research into the mental health of young people would support the adolescents' view of their happiness levels. That is, while many young people make their way through the teenage years with comparative ease and in good relationship with their parents, their teachers and their peers, there are some who find this life-stage enormously stressful.

It is these young people who are the concern of this chapter. Additionally, it is hoped that discussing the various definitions and manifestations of depression will assist parents who are confused about the significance of their particular child's visible or expressed mood.

Young People and Mental Health

Surviving the teenage years, and particularly the stresses of the Leaving Cert. Exam, requires a degree of psychological robustness. The age and stage of young people at Leaving Cert level, however, coincides with a time of particular psychological vulnerability.

Studies indicate that that the prevalence of psychiatric disorders in people aged between sixteen and twenty-five years of age has increased and that depression is likely to be in the most acute phase at this time.[1]

Firstly, there are many disorders from which adults suffer which begin in adolescence. The first signs of anxieties, of panic attacks and of obsessive-compulsive disorder, for example, often begin in the teenage years. People who suffer from social phobias often trace the origin to a significantly embarrassing incident in adolescence. Psychological distress can get translated into physical complaints, so that adolescents may complain of a relentless array of physical malaises.

Additionally, studies have shown that the common diagnoses in older teenagers are mood disorder (4.9 per cent), major depression (4 per cent), generalised anxiety (3.7 per cent), obsessive-compulsive disorder (1.9 per cent), bulimia (2.6 per cent), panic disorder (0.6 per cent), and anorexia nervosa (0.2 per cent). Also, 12 per cent of general practice attendees aged 13-19 years were found to have major depression and 6 per cent had disruptive (externalising) disorder.[2]

Furthermore, there are unacceptably high levels of alcohol consumption by students in this country, which may be an expression of the inability of young people to cope with life. Alternatively it may be the reason why those students cannot cope. Additionally, alcohol consumption is often a means by which young men in particular may try to dull the pain of their depression.

It is helpful, therefore, if parents are alert to signs that their children may need some help at this stressful Leaving Cert. time.

Awareness of depression is clearly important.

What is Depression?

The term depression is used in many and varied ways. Deciding whether or not someone is suffering from depression initially requires acquaintance with these many descriptions.[3] The following are of note:

- The term depression may describe a *mood*. Feeling 'down' at some time or other for some reason or other is a universal experience. It can be a temporary feeling of misery without any apparent cause.
- Depression may be a description of unhappiness or sadness as a *response* to life events, such as not getting on the rugby team, failing an exam or falling out with your best friend in school.
- It may refer to a personality *trait*, for example when someone is described as having a depressive personality. This is the kind of person who always appears to be pessimistic and miserable.
- Depression as an individual *symptom*, for example when someone is described as having a depressed mood.
- Depression as a *syndrome* with a series of symptoms such as insomnia, weight loss, inability to concentrate and even thoughts of suicide.
- Depression as a *disorder* or an illness It may describe a clinical condition, an illness, which includes all of the above signs at a level that may make someone lose all interest in life, capacity to work and capacity for enjoyment.
- It may describe the level of *disability* it causes, the extent to which it disables the person who is depressed, although there are some who remain apparently functional while depressed.
- Depression as a *disease*, when there is a clear genetic basis and physical signs of depression.
- Depression arising from helplessness,[4] when it seems to the depressed person that it is irrelevant what one does or does not do, there is no escape from the situation.

- Depression deriving from faulty thinking or cognitive[5] distortions that are all negative.
- Depression arising from poor social skills and a ruminative socially stressful style.[6]

In summary, being depressed or having depression may depend on the combined effects of social, psychological, and biological factors. It may include the stresses a person experiences, how that person perceives those stresses and how they are dealt with, allied to the genetic and biological resilience and capacities with which a person is originally endowed to do so.

Types of Depression

Depressions vary widely in their symptoms, their progress and their response to treatments. In the past, depressions tended to be classified fairly rigidly according to type. These descriptions helped to draw distinctions between the different ways people showed depressed mood, the different reasons why people became depressed in the first place, the intensity of the feelings and how long the feelings of depression were likely to last.

Many clinicians see depressive disorders as being along a kind of spectrum or continuum rather than rigidly divided up. This is because people do not come neatly packaged emotionally. Life is too varied, the circumstances in which people live are too vast and the life story of each person too unique for rigid classifications. However, broad categories are still useful and are as follows:

- Reactive Depression: This describes the kind of depression that occurs as a response to difficult situations or events. For example, the loss of someone, a death, failing an important exam, losing one's job or any of the many life situations that can overwhelm a person.
- Endogenous/Biological depressions. These refer to those depressions without such triggers, occurring because of some

genetic, biochemical or biological disorder. It may be difficult to identify the cause, but the symptoms are distressing.

- Manic depression. This is characterised by extremes. People with this disorder[7] may swing from misery to mania, from one emotional polarity to the other. On this emotional rollercoaster they may rise up to absolute elation and drop down to deep despair. They may have an episode in which they are euphoric, creative, manic and moving from one project to the next. This may be followed by the depths of dejection.

Identifying Depression

As noted many of the problems associated with identifying depression arise from misunderstandings about what the term depression actually means. This makes it difficult for parents to assess if the 'depressed' moods they observe in their children are transient or more serious. They wonder if the observed moods are age and stage appropriate, whether they may be connected to some life event that has upset the young person, whether the student is simply fed up with the study demands of Leaving Cert. or whether they may have a more pervasive mood disorder.

Students often say *'I'm so depressed'* when they are really describing a temporary feeling of being tired, fed up, wanting a break or wishing that something more scintillating would happen in their lives than a B on their last History assignment.

Another danger in the word 'depressed' being in ordinary parlance, is that people can think that a depressed person is merely experiencing some feelings of being 'down' over which they have control. This myth can generate devastating commands to the depressed person; *'pull yourself together'*, *'get on with it'*, *'stop feeling sorry for yourself'*, *'snap out of it'*, *'stop moping'* and *'get a life'*.

This is the last thing a depressed person can do. Indeed, because depression is usually characterised by such low self-esteem and self-loathing, the slightest suggestion of malingering or moaning, may plunge the depressed person further into the abysses of feeling misunderstood, a nuisance and a worthless parasite on the lives of others.

What to Look Out For
In view of the confusions surrounding depression, it is important for parents to know what signs and signals to look out for when trying to establish if their child may be depressed. The following descriptions may be helpful:[8]

- There may be changes, which because of their swift, intense presentation will immediately alert and alarm parents. These are in instances where a normally happy, cheerful, outgoing, optimistic, energetic, young person changes. Instead the adolescent becomes suddenly, unexpectedly unhappy, glum, withdrawn, pessimistic, lethargic, irritable and disinterested in everything.
- A change in appearance, in behaviour, in mood or in reactions is always a signal that something may be amiss, particularly if this lasts for more than two weeks.
- Any change in self-esteem is a significant signal. The adolescent whose self-esteem is poor is a much more likely candidate for depression.
- The young person may look, sad, seem sad, be tearful, be 'flat' and apathetic.
- They may have heightened sensitivity and be hurt easily by other people.
- The student may look and seem in a much worse mood in the morning, which may lift somewhat as the day progresses.
- There may be problems with the sleep pattern, which is one of the most significant indicators of depression. The student may complain about waking after a few hours sleep.
- Changes in weight may be observed. There may be weight increase with comfort eating. Alternatively, there may be

weight loss as the person loses their 'appetite' for life and for all of its pleasures.

- Loss of interest in previously enjoyed activities requires explanation and understanding.
- Signs that the person is agitated, fearful and apprehensive about life are significant.
- There can be delusions of guilt or worthlessness and self-blaming. Feelings of hopelessness about the depression ever lifting.
- There may be significant behavioural changes. Research shows that young men often act out or *externalise* their depression in difficult, disruptive, angry, aggressive, or risk taking behaviour.
- There may be signs that young women are *internalising* the problem. Their feelings of sadness may show themselves in emotional difficulties, physical and health complaints, in anxiety, in poor self-esteem or expressions of self-loathing.
- The depressed person may focus obsessively and negatively on their appearance, their body-size or shape.
- There may be relationship problems as irritable depressed students fall out with their friends or incur the wrath of their teachers for their disruptive, cheeky or oppositional behaviour.
- Correspondingly, there may be withdrawal or avoidance of social situations. The student may ruminate over whether the wrong thing was said or people were antagonised.
- Self-revulsion may reach the level that the person believes that nobody else could like or care for them.
- There may be further interpersonal problems in that parents may notice that the student's mood seems to make other people around the student unhappy. One theory[9] says that depression can affect other people's moods, which is why depressed people may have a smaller network of friends and supportive people around them.
- Look out for a slumped posture in a previously confident upright person.
- Students who are depressed often complain about poor concentration, finding it difficult to get down to tasks and having problems in decision-making.

- Parents may notice that the student seems unable to read or to absorb anything that is read.
- A student may not even be able to take in or enjoy a television programme.
- Conversely there may be a constant mindless wish to watch TV, Video or DVD late into the night.
- Expressions of pessimism and fatalism may be noted. Students may say that they are 'unlucky', 'cursed', a 'bad omen'. They may complain that *nothing ever goes right'*.
- The student may feel that they are helpless in the situation. They may make statements about the futility of study. They may say that the points system is too demanding or that the course requirements are too elevated.
- Feeling hopeless is a classic indicator. Holding the belief that good things will not happen and that bad things *will* happen regardless of what the person does.
- Parents might look out for signs of Seasonal Affect Disorder (SAD).[10] Just as the body clock regulates sleeping patterns, there may also be a 'seasonal regulator'. Parents may see significant sudden descent in mood once the days grow shorter and darker.
- Odd or unusual behaviour may be a sign of alternative non-prescription drug-taking in an adolescent. The connection between vulnerability to depression and consumption of substances has been drawn for many years.
- The student may have an endless list of physical complaints. More seriously the student may believe that they have undiagnosed serious illnesses. The hypochondriacal preoccupation with health can in turn lead to all kinds of overly attentive behaviours in relation to cleanliness and hygiene or food safety or hygiene.
- However, physical complaints should be checked. Physical ill-health can grind a student down and make everyday tasks just too difficult. Psychological distress can deplete a person physically so that disturbance in one can have an impact on the other.
- Parents may notice a manic mood, a persistently elevated, expansive or even irritable mood, inflated self-esteem,

grandiosity, big plans to save the world, to get maximum points, to change school life. There may be no need for sleep beyond a few hours and endless talkativeness with ideas being rushed out almost in incoherence.

- Parents may note terrible distractibility, where the student is attracted by the unimportant and irrelevant. There may even be signs of being physically fidgety with arms and limbs jigging and agitated.

- Parents also need to ensure that what looks like depression is not some other medical complaint. For example problems with thyroid can cause loss of vitality and lethargy, and there may be irritability, and suspiciousness. Be sure that all medical possibilities are checked out with your GP before deciding that what you are observing is depression

- Finally, because it bears repeating, there is always the possibility that changes in a young person may come about because of some organic or physical problem. These possibilities show how important it is to receive medical advice as soon as a problem is noted.

Would I Know if my Child was Depressed?

There has been a wealth of interesting research conducted in this country and elsewhere into the lives of young people. What is of particular significance in this research is that it shows how frequently and how deeply young people may be distressed and depressed while the surrounding adult world remains unaware of it. The following research papers may be of interest.

What the Research Says

Ever since the famous Isle of Wight studies by British Psychiatrist, Sir Michael Rutter[11] and his colleagues there has been research evidence of the extent to which so-called 'normal' adolescents can be upset at clinical levels in a way not observed by parents and teachers around them. Often the networks of adult authority surrounding adolescents are oblivious to the levels of internal psychological pain suffered by young people.

Of course adolescents who externalise their difficulties in disruptive or destructive conduct are more likely to come to attention, while those who suffer silently and internally may not do so.

In one 1994[12] Irish study, 464 male and female secondary school adolescents from both urban and rural locations were studied. Comparisons were made between them. One finding was that the schoolgirls from the provincial school had significantly higher psychological distress than the schoolgirls in the urban area; they showed more symptoms of depression, (22 per cent) had poorer self-esteem and were prone to feelings of guilt and self-criticism.

In this study as many as 68 per cent of the rural schoolgirls reported these feelings of poor self-esteem. This compared with more than 57 per cent of the local males, 49 per cent of Dublin females and more than 47 per cent of Dublin males who demonstrated poor self-esteem. However, if one considers these figures at a more simplistic level they suggest an unacceptably high level of self-depreciation in the young people in *both* rural and urban locations.

Whereas the study quoted above was of adolescents up to 16 years, another important Irish study.[13] by Dr Maria Lawlor and Dr Deborah James, looked at the prevalence of psychological problems in 779 older adolescents. In this study 21 per cent of adolescents had problems in the clinical range and again girls reported more problems than boys. Additionally, twice as many girls as boys reported *thinking* of suicide frequently.

Most of those who *attempt* suicide are girls, while boys predominate in *actual* suicide. This is important to note, so that the crucial and public issue of male suicide, does not overshadow the extent to which young women also have suicidal thoughts and wishes. It is also important that parents are not confused into thinking that depression in their daughters is less serious than depression in their sons. Obviously *any* young person who appears to be depressed needs urgent medical attention to relieve their distress.

Of particular interest and importance is the work of Professor

Carol Fitzpatrick[14] and her colleagues in UCD in 2001, which showed that 'suicidal thoughts are common in adolescents, and parents and teachers are usually unaware of the difficulties being experienced by such adolescents'. Another large scale study of the emotional health of young adolescents is currently underway,[15] and the initial results show that 20 per cent of school-going adolescent aged 12-15 years fall into the 'at risk' category.

This is significant information at a number of levels. It alerts parents and teachers and educationalists to the need for a psychoeducational service in secondary schools[16] and the need for significantly more adolescent support centres and accessible adolescent psychiatric services in this country.

With the high levels of distress amongst young people, creative solutions are required so that they do not have to struggle emotionally, to act out or externalise their distress, to drink alcohol to dull it, or take risks to have it attended to. The immediacy of adolescent mood and need calls for an echoed immediacy of response from all of us who work with young people.

The Leaving Cert. Student and Depression

In seeking to understand more about the young person, it is useful to consider here the many difficulties that can arise for the Leaving Cert Student. Some of these pertain specifically to the pressure and stress of study. Some problems clearly pre-exist the exam, but are exacerbated by it.

There may be difficulties, which have been lurking beneath the surface, that erupt during the Leaving Cert. year. Their origin may extend back as far as childhood, but their manifestation occurs at this critical life stage of school leaving.

Finally there may be issues that require resolution before entering into the world of adulthood, particularly struggles about independence and autonomy seeking resolution in the final year at school.

Some Stress factors

The list of what could make a student stressed, distressed or depressed may be as varied as the number of individuals undertaking Leaving Cert.

At each stage of life each person has their own unique combination of strengths, abilities and needs. Each person is likely to have areas of confidence and competence, patches of hesitancy and vulnerability and specific issues that pertain to being at that particular stage in life.

Consider the many influences on the person outlined in Chapter 2. These individual, family, social, emotional, educational, medical, psychological and cultural experiences may continue to play their part in the health and happiness of the Leaving Cert. student.

The following are also factors that make this late adolescent Leaving Cert. period particularly stressful:

- Coming from a family where there is a record of exceptional exam achievement. Sometimes this can include the extended family. Some students enter their Leaving Cert. year oppressed by high achievement levels that are beyond the particular student's scope.
- Having family members taking the same exam. This would occur in situations where a twin brother or sister or a sibling who is close in age is also doing the Leaving Cert. It is not uncommon for repeat students to have a brother or sister sitting the Leaving Cert. for the first time. What is already double pressure for the repeat student becomes multiplied.
- Filling in the CAO forms has been made as easy as such a complex process involving so many people, so many colleges and so many choices can be. Nonetheless it is a daunting task and for some students the difficulty does not lie in the mechanics of the form, but in the sudden realisation that school is ending, adult life is beginning and there are responsible choices to be made.

- Confronting one's limitations. The Leaving Cert. year leaves little room for educational difference, for learning difference or adolescent processes extraneous to the exam. It confronts students with an exam process that they must go through, although emotionally and developmentally students may be at very different stages. The student who is not ready to leave school, to make choices, to study in an organised time-managed way is personally confronted by these difficulties in a particularly forceful way.
- There are many significant events that take place during the year that require some emotional processing. For example, the school graduation ceremony can be an exceptionally emotive event. It is usually a ritual held in the school hall, in the church or on the school stage. Young people have to say good-bye to each other, good-bye to their school, good-bye to their teachers, and to an important part of their lives. Parents are usually present and are also often moved by the event. They may remember many of the young people from the time they were tiny children, friends of their own sons or daughters. The sentiments surrounding this event often do not get articulated and can make the more vulnerable adolescent feel sad or emotionally overwhelmed.
- Other events that may be emotional are the debs' dances. Once again this occasion may evoke feelings about the significance of the event. Many parents will remember their own school debutante ball and the time that surrounded it. Adolescents are not immune to their parents' nostalgia. Again, if these feelings go unexpressed and underground they can be more difficult to process.
- Adolescents who do not have a means of discharging emotion are more at risk of becoming highly stressed. Sports provide a particularly useful release of energy and emotion. Young people who play sport have the supportive connection to their teammates, the incentive of the games and the physical exercise, which assists mental health. Ironically, in the Leaving Cert. year some students decide that they do not have the time for their sports activities

and can thereby cut themselves off from a good stress releaser.

- Those young women who do not measure up to impossible criteria of attractiveness, emaciated body-size and sexualised behaviour can believe themselves to be inferior. The extent of depression in adolescent girls is not unconnected to the impossible identities that are portrayed as the norm.
- Those young men who do not have the required physical physique, strength, prowess, attractiveness and confidence can also suffer great inferiority. Having acne, having to wear glasses, needing unsightly braces or generally falling short of media generated 'perfection' imposes its own hardships on youth.
- Being unable to manage the peer group is a major cause of unhappiness at every life stage and is important at Leaving Cert. time because of the emotional outlet being part of the group provides. This requires exceptional skill in knowing the communication code, the dress code, the range of acceptable musical tastes, food preferences and acceptable venues. Where a young person socialises is now often a statement of *who* they are and what group they belong to. There is so much to learn and know in 6th year in addition to 'knowing' all these peer acceptance rules. This is difficult, especially for those who cannot grasp the codes and who are, therefore, left on the margins.
- The extent to which having material possessions, having disposable cash and possessing the trappings of adolescent power dominates adolescent culture is something that young people and their parents continue to struggle with. It places undue burden on the adolescent to work for money or on the parent to provide exorbitant 'pocket' money. It can be a source of concern or conflict and an additional stress on an already stressed system.
- There have been enormous changes in sexual mores in the past two decades. Young people are now exposed to expectations of relationship and sexual behaviour that were previously well outside the domain of adolescent

encounters. This places huge stress on them in the guise of liberation. Their construction as sexual beings, the manner in which their youth is marketed, in which they themselves are commodified and sexualised, adds to identity confusion at a critical time.

- There are highly specific problems that may arise. A student may discover that she is pregnant. Sadly, a young woman may arrange secret termination of a pregnancy, an event that can be seriously traumatic, shrouded in secrecy, and carry a high risk of depression after the event and into the years ahead.

- The Leaving Cert. year coincides with the age associated with adolescent risk-taking. Mistaken, youthful high-risk activities can have more serious consequences than adolescents anticipate when they engage in them. These can be further sources of depression when they go wrong. For example, a car accident with all the attendant stresses and financial problems. Additionally, getting into debt is not uncommon. Alternatively, many adolescents work excessively long hours for money and for entertainment.

- There may be a severe reaction to substance abuse. Correspondingly there might be an incident in which the person conducted a criminal act under the influence of alcohol and is terrified of the consequences.

- Childhood experiences may return. Young people who experienced any loss in childhood, any disruption to the normal experiences of being cared for, may show some depression at vulnerable times in adolescence and adulthood.

- Parents might like to consider if there was the loss of a partner, marital disharmony or divorce. Also, separations from the parents in childhood can make the person more anxious at the thought of separation from friends and the safety and routine of school. Partings are harder if there have previously been difficult childhood ruptures.

- Medical factors play their part. While early medical history can be a factor, parents may also consider if the student has had any recent or severe attack of 'flu' or any viral infections. Post viral depression is not uncommon and people can feel very depleted and down after a bout of illness.

- School experiences. While there is an expectation that the more extreme bullying cruelties of childhood and early adolescence should have abated by 6th year, it is a time when the more angry, vulnerable or envious may decide to vent their frustration on classmates. 'It can be difficult to determine when horseplay becomes attack, when teasing becomes treachery, when being left out becomes deliberate ostracisation or when losing friends is part of an exclusion strategy'.[17] Consider the possibility of bullying.

- It is particularly difficult for the older adolescent, the person on the verge of adulthood to admit to anyone that they are the victims of bullying. Being bullied is a dreadful assault on happiness on self-esteem and on capacity to cope and can lead to a reactive episode of depression if allowed to continue.

- Sometimes adolescents may be the recipients of the callousness of others, even their peers. The young person may have been threatened, or frightened or suffered physical assault, which they do not want to reveal to parents.

- A young woman may be raped and not know how to disclose what has happened to her. In short, students may be bullied blackmailed, intimidated or victimised in school. They may have their character impugned and not know how to deal with or redress this.

- Finally, some researchers say that depression is more likely in certain types of people, such as those who are very sensitive or introverted, those who are natural 'worriers', those who are socially 'awkward', people who are very dependent or obsessional in the behaviour they show, or those who seem insecure and prone to break down under stress.

Summary

Whatever the problem, whatever the reason, young people need support in a wide number of contexts that co-occur with Leaving Cert.

In situations where a young person feels backed into a corner, helpless to change the past or to evade the future, where there is a bleak hopelessness about life and about what lies ahead, when it seems as if there is no solution or nobody who can provide one, that is when young people may be at risk of harming themselves in some way.

What should a Parent do?

Do Not Worry

Reading a chapter about depression may worry a parent, as if depression inevitably lurks around the corner for their son or daughter. This is *not* so.[18]

What is important is that parents feel confident and competent to assess the difference between ordinary adolescent moods and transient expressions of unhappiness and more serious distress. This ensures that if intervention is required it can be got as quickly as possible.

Do Not Take Chances

We should not take chances with depression. It is better and safer to get a professional view if parents are in any doubt whatsoever about the significance of their observations.

While parents' instincts and intuition are strong when it comes to understanding their children, depression comes in too many guises and disguises and it is safer to check it out to be reassured.

Promote Self-Esteem

One of the ways that parents can help their children most is by promoting the young person's self-esteem.

Self-esteem is critical in adolescence. Having good self-esteem is the single most protective factor against most of the problems that may befall the young person. With self-esteem intact young people are more able to resist peer pressure, the courage of alcohol is not required for social situations, drugs may be resisted.

Conversely, having poor self-esteem is at the core of many adolescent problems. An adolescent with poor self-esteem is plagued by doubt about self, about identity, about relationship with others, about how to behave in the group and about how to resist peer group. Poor self-esteem makes a young person feel that they are unattractive, that they are stupid, that they have little value and no worth. Thereafter, the young person begins to enumerate all the reasons why acceptance by others cannot be achieved.

Parents, who can promote self-esteem in every possible situation, go a long way towards helping their adolescent.

Other Factors

Parents may also wish to attend to the following for their Leaving Cert students:

- Ensure that the Leaving Cert. student is academically and intellectually capable of what he or she is undertaking. Realistic expectations of and by the young person are important. If they are not realistic they need to be altered.
- Look out for signs of stress during the year and introduce the stress reducers outlined in Chapter 8.
- Assist in time management if the young person will allow that. Parents are referred to Chapter 6.
- Attend to physical complaints, but try to help the adolescents from using illness as a way of avoiding difficulties.
- Attend to cosmetic needs that would help the young person's confidence. For example, consult a dermatologist if acne is unsightly, an orthodontist if teeth protrude and in so far as possible be sympathetic to the importance of appearance in the mind of the young person.

- Encourage friends and friendships and the means by which the young person may participate on an equal footing. This means being generous within the parameters of common sense, ensuring that the young person has 'enough' of the clothes and gear and pocket money that allow inclusion into the group.
- Praise for the young person's appearance is important. It is a great confidence boost as they leave the house to meet their friends.
- Provide, if possible, the assistance they need in their studies, e.g. a grind in a difficult subject.
- It may be opportune to review the core issues that the Leaving Cert. students suggested. These are outlined in Chapter 5. If possible parents might attend to some of those suggestions of what would help the student during this year.
- Most importantly parents can help their child when they *listen attentively to their concerns*, respect their worries and do *not* provide false reassurances. These 'reassurances', which adolescents experience as a parental cut-off, can particularly prevent young people disclosing their worries or distress.

Conclusions

Most students will experience some anxiety at some stage during the Leaving Cert. year. Indeed, a small measure of adrenalin is usually required to get moving and motivated. If academic goals don't inspire, sometimes a small dose of anxiety does.

But because there is an expectation that students may be somewhat stressed during the Leaving Cert. year the level of their stress may get overlooked. The classic signals of depression, such as fatigue, anxiety, irritability or occasional sleeplessness arising from the pressure of study may be misconstrued. Stress may be mistaken for depression and depression may be mistaken for stress.

The danger of this is that significant psychological and psychiatric distress may not be taken seriously and be diminished or dismissed as moodiness, irritability, anger, panic or depression about the Leaving Cert. in instances where the exam is irrelevant. This may leave the depressed student grappling, unattended with the misery of a depressed condition.

Furthermore, it may bring about the situation where the Leaving Cert. is considered to have 'caused' the eventually identified depression rather than being the end-point, the final straw or the catalyst for an adolescent who was already struggling.

But ironically, having 'something' to blame can sometimes do the opposite and be exceptionally useful.

There are adolescents out there for whom the Leaving Cert. was the necessary catalyst for change and attention to their difficulties. Adolescents, who finally told their parents how helpless, lonely, inadequate or depressed they were feeling, because they didn't know how to do so earlier. Adolescents whose depression might not have been noticed were it not for the Leaving Cert.

There are parents, too, who had been worried about their sons or daughters for a long time, who finally found a way of helping them, under the guise of exam stress.

In summary, the Leaving Cert. may obstruct recognition of an adolescent's depression or may be the mechanism by which a depressed adolescent finally receives attention.

It is important that it serves the latter purpose.

Notes

1   Rutter, M. & Smith, D.J. (eds) (1995) *Psycho-social disorders in young people: Time Trends and their Causes,* John Wiley and Son, London.
2   Whitaker et al (1990) and Kramer and Garralda (1998), cited in Stanley and Manthorpe (2002) *Students' Mental Health Needs,* Jessica Kingsley, London.
3   Angold, A. (1988) 'Childhood and Adolescent Depression Epidemiological and Aetiological Aspects', *Journal of Psychiatry,* 152, 601-617.

4   Abramsom, L.Y., Metalsky, G.I. & Alloy, L.B. (1989) 'Helplessness Depression: A theory based subtype of depression', *Psychological Review* 96, 358-372.

5   Beck, A.T., Rush, A.J., Shaw, B.F., and Emery, G. (1979) *Cognitive Therapy of Depression,* Guildford, New York.

6   Lewinsohn, P.M., Roberts, R.E., Seeley, J.R., Rohde, P., Gotlib, I.H. and Hops, H. (1994) 'Adolescent Psychopathology: 11 Psychosocial Risk Factors for Depression', *Journal of Abnormal Psychology* 103, 302-315.

7   There is interesting research into the high incidence of bipolar disorders or manic-depression in significant artists, composers, writers, musicians and inventors. Perhaps the downside of the capacity to feel extremely is the crippling extremes of feeling to be endured. See also Jamison, K.R. (1997) *An Unquiet Mind: A Memoir of Moodiness and Madness*, Random House, New York.

8   Medical attention should be sought if parents have any concern about a young person being depressed.

9   Gotlib, I. H. & Lee, C.M. (1989) 'The social functioning of depressed patients: A longitudinal assessment', *Journal of Social and Clinical psychology* 8, 223-237.

10 Terman M., Terman, J.S. Quitkin, F.M. et al (1989) 'Light therapy for seasonal affective disorder: A review of efficacy' *Neuropsychopharmacology* 2, 1-22.

11 Rutter, M, Tizard, J., Yule, W., Graham, P., & Whitmore, K. (1976) 'Isle of Wight Studies 1964-1974' *Psychol. Medicine* 6, 313-332.

12 Houlihan, B., Fitzgerald, M. & O'Regan, M (1994) 'Self Esteem, depression and hostility in Irish adolescents', *Journal of Adolescence* 17, 565-577.

13 Lawlor, M. & James, D. (2000) 'Prevalence of psychological problems in Irish schoolgoing adolescents', *Irish Journal of Psychological Medicine* 17, (4) 117-122.

14 Rowley, J., Ganter, K., & Fitzpatrick, C. (2001) Suicidal thoughts and acts in Irish Adolescents. *Irish Journal of Psychological Medicine* 18, 82-86.

15 Lynch, F., Mills, C., Daly, I. & Fitzpatrick, C. (2002) *Challenging Time: coping with life stress in childhood and adolescence.* (Presentation to the Royal College of Psychiatrists Conference, Harrogate, September 2002).

16 Most recent information from the Department of Education and Science is that by 2003, the five-year plan of having a designated educational psychologist to all schools will have been completed.

17 Murray, M. & Keane, C. (1998), *The ABC of Bullying*, RTÉ/Mercier Press, Cork.
18 Figures suggest approx 5 per cent of 12-18 year olds suffer from depressive disorders. While 20 per cent may be emotionally unhealthy that means 80 per cent are coping most of the time. We need to be aware, not worried.

11

THE LAST FEW WEEKS –
UNDERSTANDING THE STUDENT

Tensions increase for everyone as exam time approaches. The reality and the imminence of the exam hit home. There is so little time left; yet it is sufficient if that time is used appropriately. Each day is significant. Intense application to study can still make a big different to the final result at this stage. This fact alone causes tension.

Parents say that the young person's role and obligation at this stage is to study to the best of their capacity for the limited remaining time. Parents who do not observe their offspring showing appropriate commitment understandably become worried. *'After all,'* they say, *'if they can't get down to study now, even at this late stage, then there is no hope for them.'*

Meanwhile, other parents worry about the intensity of their child's study pattern fearing that such momentum of study cannot be sustained and that the student will be burnt-out or stressed-out before the actual exam begins.

Still other parents are pleased that their children seem to have hit a balance of good study patterns and social life and know that it is just a matter of holding steady through the remaining weeks and the exam itself and the strain of the year will soon be over.

All in all, these last weeks are anxious times for most as parents find themselves parenting different kinds of students who are showing different studying styles.

How Students Study in the Last Weeks

The 'Apathetic' Student

There are parents who wish their student would just show some recognition of the seriousness of the event ahead. These parents listen to media reports of 'stressed-out students' with incredulity, derision or even envy and think that in their own child's case a little stress wouldn't go astray. They would welcome even a morsel of motivation or intention to study *something* before the exam begins. .

It is important not to be angry or resentful of the young person who has not managed to get down to study. It is helpful if parents look on this behaviour as a sign of their immaturity and lack of readiness rather than one of defiance or laziness. Parents need to remember that the appearance of indifference may be covering up anxiety about failure. Irritability, touchiness and anger are often signs of stress and depression

The 'Anxious' Student

Parents who watch their children become stressed and anxious are understandably concerned. When the anxiety of the student is expressed as an inability to study, this is even more alarming. It increases the anxiety. It decreases the capacity to study. Each day is a day nearer to the exam, which exacerbates both anxiety and inability.

As anxiety and immobility compound each other, parents themselves may become immobilised for fear that their interventions might tip the balance in their child's fragile state.

The 'Compulsive' Student

Parents worry when they watch their child become obsessed with study to the exclusion of almost all other activities. When a young person increases their study hours and exhibits extreme anxiety, anger or irritability at any suggestion of 'taking a break', this concerns parents at a number of levels. There is fear that the young person will 'crack up' or 'have a nervous breakdown'.

Sometimes parents of the obsessive student listen to the complaints of other parents about 'lazy', 'de-motivated' students, who are more committed to social life than study and secretly wish their child would take a night off.

The Regular Student
There are parents whose children have applied themselves reasonably well to their studies throughout the year. These parents are uncertain about what, if anything, they should do at this stage in the year. They are torn between encouragement and encroachment into the student's routine. On the one hand, if students appear to be studying, perhaps they should be left to their own devices. On the other hand, the parents feel obliged to advise that stepping the study up a gear might maximise the benefits of the weeks ahead.

Finally, many parents find, at this stage of the year, that their children are doing the best that they can and they wonder how they can help the young person to maximise the time available to them.

Parental Responses

This is the time to make decisions based on what kind of student your own child is. Student anxiety requires one set of responses, apathy another and depression yet another response.

Students showing marked changes in patterns of eating, or of sleeping, students who are having nightmares, students who look unhappy, whose mood is flat or miserable are sending a signal of difficulty in coping. A clinically depressed student needs immediate medical attention.

Equally, students who become uncharacteristically abrasive, who look angry and permanently irritated are not coping well. Irritability at this stage in the year is not unusual as the pressure piles up and the time runs out. But irritability is also always a signal that something is wrong, so parents need to keep an eye on it, particularly if it is out of character or exaggerated.

Other students may somatise their difficulties and produce a range of physical complaints. It is important that complaints of physical illness are listened to at this and every stage in the year. Additionally, if a student cannot find another way of achieving attention, this is an important message to all the adults around the student that the whole exam has become too much.

Some students get so overwrought that they return to 'headless' behaviour, switching from one task to the next, appearing downstairs every few minutes. They cannot focus. They cannot concentrate. They waste time and energy. Sometimes getting back to the basics of preparing a place, a space and a study plan is what they need. It is also important to remember that students who are showing some level of poor concentration may be stressed. Most definitely they need help.

If the student is apathetic parents can try to motivate him or her by suggesting some of the study guides outlined below for these final few weeks. But parents always need to remember that they cannot study for another person, they can only provide the conditions that are regarded as most conducive to study. After that it is a learning process for both parents and offspring.

It may be irritating and disappointing in the extreme for parents to find that despite every help and privilege their particular child cannot or will not study. If that continues there may be reasons, other than academic ones, which will require some professional intervention. Stress and distress are also often masked by apathy.

Whatever the student is displaying in these last weeks, parents' observations are important. This is the time when parental vigilance is crucial in order to respond to whatever message a student is trying to convey about their capacity or inability to cope.

Helping Students with Lifestyle – Points for Parents

In addition to the many study strategies on which parents will advise their children, the following lifestyle and healthy approaches to study are also necessary at this time. Parents may wish to advise their children on the following:

- Students need to eat well and sensibly. A good breakfast is crucial, an adequate lunch and early dinner and not too many junk or sugar surges.
- Walk and exercise. It is obvious, but important. If you can afford it and there is a health club nearby, this is a good year to take out membership for the student. Swimming is a particularly de-stressing and helpful whole-body exercise. Students often literally wash their troubles away with a swim.
- Alcohol is not conducive to proper stress-management or study-efficiency. Up to two days can be lost by turning to it as a source of reassurance, escape or courage.
- Study is hard work. At this time it is the student's most important job. This is, therefore, the time to suspend or give up part-time jobs. No one can manage the amount of concentrated study needed in addition to work commitments.
- A sensible sleeping pattern is important and serves students well in the run up to exams. If students have fallen into any habits such as studying late and sleeping late in the morning that sleep-wake cycle needs to be changed to the one needed during the exams. The way to establish a good pattern is to get up early every day, regardless of fatigue, until the pattern is back to 'early to bed early to rise'.
- Students need to choose nights out with activities and friends that will guarantee they will be home early enough to get a good night's sleep. This is not the time to go out until late at night at the weekend.
- It often relieves worry and stress if students articulate their concerns. Students may like to write out their worries before

they begin studying. Externalising problems by writing them down helps to release them from the mind. In other words, generalised anxieties usually get translated into specific, solvable problems when written down.

- Warm, milky drinks at night can assist sleep. A selection of nourishing snacks stops the student snacking too often on sugary foods.
- Help the student to reduce coffee and caffeine intake, as this does not assist study.
- Parents can help students by suggesting hot, refreshing showers. Some parents like to provide treats such as a token for a day at the health club where swimming, a sauna or Jacuzzi can cheer and revive. Alternatively, as suggested above, an entire year's membership allows a routine of study and healthy exercise. Or what about providing some very special and refreshing toiletries? Perhaps some to relax, some to refresh and some to revive?
- Some parents may pay for a session of reflexology, aromatherapy, biofeedback, acupuncture or massage or other medically indicated stress-management techniques.
- Students are advised to use any relaxation strategies they choose on a regular basis, particularly to help sleep at night. Yoga, mood-creating tapes, environmental sounds, soothing music – whatever works should be used.
- The old remedies for stress – a hot bath, warm milk, a cosy, warm relaxing bedroom and bed and a regular pattern of sleep – are still valid.
- Some students like to use essential oils, such as lavender for calm and sleep, chamomile tea for relaxation or other herbal teas and rescue-remedies. They should seek medical advice to ensure that there are no medical contraindications to any new substance being tried.
- Sitting hunched over desks can cause muscles in neck, shoulders and back to tense. Teeth and jaws may clench and the body becomes alert in the 'fight or flight' mode. Suggest that the students try clenching and unclenching muscles to relieve them. They should start with toes and work their way

mentally through all the muscles, feeling the difference between the tense, clenched and the unclenched muscles.

- Lavendar-filled pillows and backrests that heat up in the microwave can help ease muscles cramped from leaning over desks. Also, placing the heated pillow on the feet can be very reviving. These pillows are relatively inexpensive; alternatively, a large sock filled with uncooked rice and heated in the microwave for 15-20 seconds works well. Some parents advise the student to sit with a back support of cushions or pillows when studying.
- If the tongue is attached to the palate the student is stressed. Suggest that your child checks this regularly. It is a barometer of tension.
- Stress can also be measured by placing fingers and hand against the face. If the hand is *not* as warm as the face it is a sign of tension. Cold hands are also often a stress indicator. This can be helped by students imagining their hands in a basin of hot water, which warms them and releases tension. It is interesting how effective this can be as a relaxation exercise.
- Students who learn to take care of themselves physically and mentally during the exam period are learning an important lesson.

Finally, students also need to be reminded, not to get stressed about being relaxed. A balance in all things is a good mental health strategy.

12

THE LAST WEEKS – HEAD INTO THE EXAM

If there is no learning without revision, there is no exam without rehearsal. Understanding, learning, memorising and revising are but a part of the process. The crucial time is the three hours in which the student must convey what he or she knows in a clear, succinct, relevant and readable manner.

Of course, the Mocks provide an opportunity for students to make mistakes, misread questions, mistime questions, misunderstand instructions or even neglect to read the entire exam paper. That is the great value of exam conditions. It is why all revision at this late stage in the year should be focused almost entirely on becoming familiar and proficient in planning answers to previous examination questions.

In other words, every study session should now be a revision and an examination preparation session. How does this work?

Helping Students Revise With the Exam in Mind

As students read and re-read examination papers, they will notice that there are specific formats to the questions asked in each subject and the number of questions to be attempted. They need to become so familiar with this that when they sit down to the examination they will know exactly what style of paper to expect. They must know how many questions on what range of topics is usually required. They should have practised providing those kinds of answers.

They should, of course have TIMED themselves doing so. They should have worked out in advance how many minutes they can allocate per question.

As students study in this way, they will be surprised at how much they actually know. They will be reassured as they develop their ability to communicate this knowledge, and become familiar with answering styles. They will find that spending time planning is important. For example, English essays are much less unwieldy if planned. Students should prepare opening sentences for topics, note the important points they want to make and make those points paragraph by paragraph. They need to decide what opinions they hold on a range of topics so that if those topics are amongst the essay options provided in the exam, the student will have already established a view, a reason for that opinion and an ability to argue the pros and cons of the subject.

As students revise with questions in mind, they will begin to know when to provide bullet points and when to provide more elaborate text. They will learn how to read a paper, how to make a choice of the questions they want to answer and how to set about answering the question.

When students mentally compose answers to exam questions they may encounter material they do not know or cannot remember. Anything a student cannot remember *now*, is a blessing. There is time to learn it and know it on the day of the exam. *This* is the time to test memory and re-commit anything that has been forgotten to memory.

Students will also find that the best way to revise Maths is to keep solving mathematical problems and ensuring that they understand what they are doing. They need to mentally bring themselves through experiments in Science.

They need to recall historical events, what led up to them, who the principal players were and how the situations were resolved or ended. They may follow the exciting journeys of heroes and gods in Classical Studies. They should prepare answers to Social and Scientific questions. They should compose French, German, Spanish, Italian or other language essays in their minds, choosing impressive phraseology, captivating opening sentences and a series of exquisite words with which to make their points in that language. These will be well rehearsed, so that they will know exactly when and where to produce them.

They should be as comfortable with the process of examinations as they can be, because they will have prepared themselves well mentally. There is time to do so if all systems go.

It is Never Too Late to Get Started

Whatever has happened up to this time, these last few weeks are important. This is the time to set aside the past and look to the future. This is the time for students to get reorganised, get studying and get whatever help they need to make their way successfully through the weeks ahead.

This is a time when you, their parents, can be exceptionally helpful. One way of helping may be to provide them with study tips and advice from which you may wish to select some of the following:

- *Don't panic.* It is important not to panic. There is still time. But it is time to do a number of things – get organised, get studying, get whatever help is needed.
- *Don't get overwhelmed.* This is the time when people say, *'I can't, I'm panicking, It's too late, It's no use, I'm dead'.* That is never the case. It is amazing how much students can learn in a short time, particularly with the wonderful, young brains they have during their teens.
- *Get organised.* If notes are still not in order, that is the first thing to be attended to. Get a cardboard box per subject or buy the large, coloured, plastic storage boxes that can be used again. Assign a different colour to each subject. Label them. Into each box put all the notes and books from that particular subject and sort them out. These boxes 'contain' the subject, in every sense of the word. It is a physical filing system that helps the mental filing system.

- *Find and file.* A crucial part of being organised is finding and filing everything, books, videotapes, newspaper cuttings on essay topics, everything connected to a subject should be put in the box allocated to that subject.
- *Gather all essays and written assignments.* If one considers all the work that may go into preparing an essay, it is a shame not to use that work. Students are advised to gather all their essays and written assignments in the different subjects that have been done throughout the school year, particularly if they were praised. Homework is the collation of ideas in a structured form. Students should also look at the suggestions or corrections that their teachers made. Those comments or corrections represent good advice on either what to do, or what not to do, when answering that question in an exam situation. Often an essay that a student has written can be memorised and form the basis of an answer in the Leaving Cert. exam. Such assignments are usually remembered more easily because the student originally composed them.
- *Organise physical space.* If allocating or organising a definite physical space hasn't already happened it needs to be done *now*. This is the time to designate a specific place to study and establish a routine of going there, and only there, to study. Good lighting and correct room temperature are also important.
- *Desk, not bed.* Studying on the bed can induce sleep. Alternatively, it can prevent sleep at night when study and bed become too closely interlinked mentally.
- *Exercise.* Students often get cold sitting in one place, so excess artificial heat is turned on. This may cause headaches and excessive heat is also very tiring. Heat from exercise is best, so a few quick exercises at intervals is advised. A walk is one of the best ways of clearing the brain, energising the body and sending students back to the books truly refreshed.
- *Eye exercises.* Eyes can become tired. It is recommended that students look out the window or into the distance at intervals, rotate neck, swing arms and loosen up. This helps fatigue and concentration.

- *Study milieu.* This is the stage when it is important to create a study milieu that matches the exam situation. For this reason students are advised *not* to listen to music while studying. They need to recreate the silence of exam conditions. While music does not interrupt the intake of information, it does affect the retrieval of that information. We remember best in situations that exactly match the situation in which we studied.
- *Get studying.* Students may need to make a new study plan based on the number of subjects that they are taking in the Leaving Cert. and the number of days per subject that remain before the exam begins.
- *Allocate time.* Allied to the point above, if there are approximately four weeks left, if you are sitting seven subjects, that's a max of four days per subject.
- *Follow the plan.* Students should know exactly what they are going to do when they sit down to study.
- *Develop study patterns.* While some breaks and leisure time should be factored in to a student's timetable, this is a time for strong study patterns. It is the final countdown and the time to make study the priority and give it all the attention the student can give.
- *Review curriculum.* Students who are studying in a haphazard fashion need to find out exactly what is prescribed in each subject. If there are sections of the curriculum with which the student is unfamiliar, this may be the time to choose to omit these sections and concentrate on knowing other sections well. In order to do this, students need to understand the options that are given in the exam and ensure that they cover enough to allow them an option in each section of an exam paper.
- *Scrutinise exam papers.* Students should examine past papers, discover the patterns and the format of questions. How are the questions asked? Could the student answer them?
- *Draw up exam question lists.* Allied to above, make a list of all those previous questions or question types in each subject area. It is helpful if these are highlighted in the books of past papers. As noted, these should be used as a study guide.

- *Revision books.* If a student has left things to the last minute, then this is the time to buy the revision books. Many are excellent and help students become familiar with all the relevant material on the course. It should be stressed that this is *not* the recommended path to education, but the recommended path to examinations.
- *Colour coding.* Students should not be afraid to write on these revision books. This is the time to use different coloured highlighters for the different subjects. The colour used will depend on the colour that the student decided at the start of the year to allocate to that subject. The box in which material is being organised should also be in the colour that has been allocated to that subject. This colour coding helps the filing system of the brain.
- *Teach to remember.* One of the best ways of remembering material is to explain it to another person. Students can elicit their parents' help in this by having them listen to an account of poems, plays, history of art, science experiments or maths problems.
- *Avoid interruptions.* It is important that students do not allow interruptions to their study at this stage. Friends can be contacted between 8 and 9 p.m. or at a specified time. Mobile phones should be left off during study times.
- *Just start for ten minutes.* Students finding it difficult to get down to study need to remember the maxim of 'just go in for ten minutes'. If they get themselves into the room to study they are likely to stay there, particularly if they have a study plan.
- *Performance enhancers.* Rosemary oil is meant to help memory. It reportedly connects the two times, the study time and the test time, so that what is learnt in one instance is recollected in the other. Apart from this, many students say that they find it pleasant and reassuring. If students are going to use this, it is important to do so while studying and also to bring some to the exam. This can be done by putting a few drops on cotton wool or a sleeve cuff.
- *Draw maps.* Revise with diagrams, spidergrams, get index cards or special revision notebooks. This is the time to put

points into revisable chunks, making sure that the writing is large, clear and ready for the LAST MINUTE REVISION that will take place during the exams.

- *Mind Mapping.* Students who have used Tony Buzan's[1] Mind-Mapping Techniques should gather all their maps for the different subjects at this stage and revise directly from them.
- *Plan answers.* All revision at this stage of the year should take the form of planning answers to questions. This is not the time to study in broad generalities. This is the time to make every bit of study be in the service of answering a possible examination question. Students are advised to write out such a list of potential exam questions.
- *Compose possible exam answers.* Having drawn up a list of possible questions, it is not necessary to write out full answers, although occasional practise in doing so is good exam preparation. Students can also simply jot down the points they *would* make if they were answering a particular exam question.
- *Practise writing at speed.* Students should get used to writing continuously for forty-five minutes without a break. This is the usual time devoted to one question in many exams.
- *Compose mental answers.* Some students mentally compose answers. They imagine what they would write if they were in the exam situation answering a particular question.
- *Dictate answers.* Other students use a Dictaphone into which they dictate the answer they would write. This allows the student to listen back for the clarity of their answer and to check for omissions.
- *Study reviews.* It is important at the end of every study session to mentally review what has been studied. Ask what has been learnt in this study session. This can be very reassuring for students. Alternatively, if there is little that has been learnt because of switching and chopping and changing subjects, then it is time for the student to review their approach to study.
- *Learning methods.* Experiment with and discover your own preferred method of committing information to memory.

Some students like to read, others to listen, some to speak the words aloud, others to repeat them or chant them. Some students learn by seeing a diagram, a map or a picture. Others learn by watching a video, bringing together the sound and sight of the information to assist their understanding and recall. Students should find out how they learn best or in what combination of learning techniques. Study that way as much as possible.

- *Taking time.* This is the time of the year to ensure that time that could be used in the service of study is not wasted. Students can mentally go over questions at odd times, for example, while waiting for a bus, sitting at the dentist, waiting for a TV programme. We gather up to two hours miscellaneous time in any one day. That's a lot of revision opportunities.

- *Study with others.* It is useful to have some study sessions with equally interested peers. It can be reassuring – and much less lonely – to revise occasionally with friends. Some companionship is a good antidote to stress. Other students may remember important points in a subject that have been forgotten. Also, the sharing of perspectives brings a richness of ideas. Studying with others allows the student to listen to talk, to write, to learn in a variety of ways rather than in silent solitary study.

Practical Parental Help

While the student is using many of the above techniques, parents too can help their children in a number of practical ways.

- Firstly they can work with the student on some of the tasks outlined above. For example, they can help the student get organised or re-organised, providing a place to study and all the revision books and exam papers and study aids that would help at this late stage in the year.

- If the student wishes to revise by talking about a subject, being a willing listener is supportive. This is not the time to criticise or interrupt.
- Reading essays or exam questions the student has composed shows that you are interested in their work and is very encouraging, but only if they ask you to.
- Invite students to explain a concept, tell you the plot of a novel, the themes in a poem, how to solve a maths problem. Teaching brings clarity and assists memory.
- Keeping noise levels in the house down. Younger children playing music, entertaining friends or listening to TV can be very disruptive.
- Contain irritability. Be a bit lenient if the young person is irritable.
- The odd snack or warm drink is very heart-warming to the student.
- Some brightly covered notebooks often cheer a student up.
- Help chaos management. This may be a time to enter the chaos of the adolescent's bedroom or study room and clean it or help to keep it clean. It is hard to study in a physically cluttered space.
- Help the young person to keep too many phone calls or interruptions at bay.
- Suggest an evening walk before study or after it.
- Look out for signs of stress and offer support.
- This is also the time to relieve the young person of most household tasks and to actively reward their study efforts by trying to make life as pleasant as possible.
- This is also the time to ask if there are any ways you can help. This is not the time to induce guilt.
- It is important to be sympathetic. If the student has not studied then help is needed now to rescue the situation.
- Resist the *'I told you so'*, *'You've left it too late'*, *'If only you had just studied all year,'* or even *'Now you are learning the hard way'*.
- Keep an eye on your own stress. One stressed out Leaving Cert. student is enough stress for any household.

Finally, parents can help their children to keep perspective on the Leaving Cert. as *one* measure of *one* aspect of a person's ability in prescribed areas and not a measure of the person.

Notes

1   Buzan, T. (2001) *Headstrong: How to get physically and mentally fit,* Thorsons, London.

13

THE EXAM

What's done is done. The time has come. The exams have begun.

Most parents and students greet the arrival of the actual exams with a mixture of anxiety and relief. Worry about the weeks ahead; relief that the end is in sight.

It is of course an anxious time. Those who have studied well are anxious that nothing happens to prevent their hard work paying off. They hope that no unanticipated accident, illness or injury afflicts them or anyone belonging to them. They know how important it is to keep focused and to make their way steadily through the exam days ahead. They have studied. They have revised. Now is the time to show what they know.

There will be other students who were not able to study. Some students who were not yet mature enough for the process. They were chronologically too young, emotionally too young or generally too immature for this exam this year. Its time for them to do the best they can at this stage.

There are always some students who sabotage themselves, being unable or unwilling to make the sacrifices required for an exam year. This can be a salutary lesson; the lesson that there is only so much a parent can do after which students must take responsibility for themselves.

There will be students whose family problems took centre stage, where family circumstances may have conspired against them, who will be trying to rescue some results from the situation.

Some students may have hit special circumstances, may have become stressed or depressed and too unwell to study. If parents and students have weathered this together this is something to be proud of. It is important to validate those students who were able to identify their difficulties, know their needs, seek help and avail of intervention. They have already passed an important life test.

In summary, there will be the students who studied, the students who didn't, the students who couldn't and the students who wouldn't. All now face into the same assessment. It is not over until it is over. It is not over yet. Managing the exam is the next crucial step.

The Day Before the Exam

On the day before the exam the student is usually at home with the entire day to study English. The Leaving Cert. has traditionally begun with English. It is, therefore, worth saying a little specifically about this because of its importance as a Leaving Cert. paper and psychologically as the first paper of the exam.

Studying for the English Paper

The day before the Leaving Cert. exam, students naturally feel compelled to study only English. There is usually a limit to how much the student who has already studied the English course can revise in this subject without becoming muddled. It is better to just check over revision notes in a calm way.

- Gentle revision using the spidergrams, or mind-maps, (see Chapter 4) can help sort and categorise information rather then amalgamate it in a muddle. Maybe making a map of the themes in poems, points on different essay topics or the characteristics of characters in the prescribed play or novel.
- The English 'essay' is a significant part of the paper. This is a mixed blessing. On the one hand, there are limits to the

preparation that can be done for an essay, which could be on almost any topic under the sun. An essay is written on the spot on the day. On the other hand, because anxiety can usually be relieved by study, it is harder for the student who feels vulnerable in English to prepare.

- Of course, there is some preparation in the art of essay writing. Information on a range of topics may have been collated. Views and opinions may have been clarified in advance. Students may have collated a range of useful, generic quotes that can be used in all contexts. Maybe some good openers and summaries have been designed that have universal applicability. Students can look over these if they have them. There is time the day before to prepare some if they have not done so. Also spending time flicking through a dictionary can help revive the student's vocabulary and creative use of words.
- But essentially the essay calls for the student's own creative processes. Those with a love of English, of reading, of constructing their ideas will feel comfortable about this. Those for whom this is their least proficiency will not, particularly those with SLDs as outlined in Chapter 9.
- Furthermore, there would appear to be a gender difference in attitude toward the first day of the Leaving because it is the English exam. The well-researched, general precocity of young women in language vis-à-vis the precocity of young men in visual-spatial and mathematical reasoning[1], means that there are different dreads for different students on different days. English has been found to be generally more anxiety provoking for males than females.
- If English is not a student's best subject, then there is no point in the student getting psyched-out by it. If it is a student's favourite subject, chances are that will show itself in the exam tomorrow if the student remains calm.
- What is most important, on the day before the exam, is that the student spends it in a way that makes him or her feel most confident and energised. It may be watching videotapes of the course material. It may be listening to

music to get in the creative mood. It may be talking to friends on the phone.

- Talking to friends is particularly important the day before the Leaving Cert. It reassures the student of the normality of their concerns and it can even make the event seem like an adventure.
- As students vacillate between excitement and anxiety, a sense of importance and a sense of dismay, it is better that they do so in the company of their friends than alone at home. Whatever keeps the student calm and connected to the Leaving Cert. process the day before it, is to be encouraged.

Practical Preparation

It is a good idea to prepare a list of practical tasks some weeks before the exam. These can then be carried out on the day before and ticked off as each one is completed. Of course, lists are personal and could include anything from visiting the mosque, church or synagogue for last minute entreaties to higher powers, to phoning Granny or Aunt Mabel to tell them you are okay.

Whatever the student's tasks the day before, they should be written down. Lists remove anxieties from the mind and transpose them into practical tasks on a page. Most lists will include some of the following:

- Sorting out clothes. Having everything ready for the next day. It is best to wear layers of clothes to an exam, to allow for temperature changes or draughty exam halls, or overly sunlit venues. Then garments can be put on or removed to keep the student comfortable. Most school uniforms are designed this way, but the non-uniform student should consider comfort as well as style. Both help confidence.
- If a student is going to use revision cards, mind-maps or notes in the morning or on the way to the exam they should

be prepared and packed. Anything the student thinks they may want to look over at the last minute should be packed, but accessible, in the morning.

- All exam accoutrements, pencil-case, pens, should be gathered early in the day so that anything overlooked can be purchased without panic. However, this is not the time to give the student a new pen or pencil case. What is familiar is more reassuring. It is what the student will have studied with. Also, new pens can take a bit of time to run in. If new implements are to be bought this should be a month or so prior to the exam.
- Bus money, or lunch money should be packed. If a parent is preparing a packed lunch for the student, a few extra treats, a bar of chocolate, food they particularly enjoy can be added. A bit of extra lunch money also won't go astray.
- If the student is lucky enough to have a mobile phone, this should be powered up the day before so that the student won't be upset if it is out of power in the morning. A phone can be useful if a student who is travelling alone to the exam hits a problem, such as a delayed bus or forgetting something vital. However, the student needs to remember to switch it off before the exam. If your child does not have a mobile phone, remember the generations of children who got the Leaving Cert. exam successfully without one.
- Parents should ask their own friends and relations who may send a card to the student, or who may phone with good wishes, to do so a few days before the exam. Too much hype the day before or on the morning of the exam can make some students anxious.
- Students should make sure they know *exactly* what time the exam begins and *exactly* where their exam is being held. This may sound obvious, but it is surprising how many students over the years have gone in at the wrong time, or to the wrong place or for the 'wrong' subject. While it is unlikely to happen on the first day, it *has* happened. More importantly, keep a check on morning or afternoon exams as the Leaving Cert. progresses.

- This is the stage when the timetable of the exams and dates on which they are taking place can be prominently displayed above the students' desk and downstairs in the kitchen, so that there are double checks on the schedule in the days and weeks ahead.

The Night Before the Exam

An important part of managing the exam is managing the night before the first exam, when the hype is at its highest and stress hurdles seem too high. This is an important time for parents to be around as much as possible, if they can. Being home in the evening for a warm evening meal is reassuring as this is the time when tension is likely to be highest.

- It is good to remind your child that most students find that the exams are not as bad as they anticipated. It is the build up that is the worst.
- Also remind the student not to focus on what he or she does not know, as people often know much more than they realise. At this stage, it is about making the most of what the student does know.
- Obviously this is not the time to admonish the student who really has not worked during the year. If the student admits this, parents might say in a calm and reassuring voice. 'yes, you didn't or couldn't get down to it, but at this stage why not give it your best shot. If it doesn't work you'll know for the future what has to be done'. There really is no point in lectures the night before the exam. Afterwards, there can be full discussion of why the student couldn't, or wouldn't, study and what needs to be done.
- Some students who have studied well are afraid they won't remember all they have learned. Again parents can remind them that 'its easier to remember when you have to answer a specific question'. Ask the student if it would help if you asked them specific questions from the Leaving Cert. papers.

Remind them about the remarkable memories people their age usually have and especially that their memory will kick in when they sit down to the exam.

- You could also tell them about the research that shows that the normal stress people feel when they sit down to an exam makes the brain much more efficient and usually brings back what has been learned.
- Students may start voicing their worries about having enough time to write down what they know, particularly the night before the English exam, which has a big writing commitment. This is an opportunity for parents to remind them that everyone has the *same* time and that it is *what* is written, not how much that is important. Tell them to keep their sentences simple, short and to the point.
- One way students often express the pre-exam nerves is by wandering aimlessly about the house. Students often do this the night before the exam. What they really want is a bit of company and reassurance. This is not the night to send them up to study.
- This is a good time to be around and chat to the young person about life in general, to go for a walk and to help them engage in a relaxed routine for the day ahead. It is a good night to have a hot bath, warm milk, (which has a sedative effect) and a few drops of lavender on the pillow to help relax.
- Sometimes when a parent asks a student, the night before the Leaving Cert., if they are okay or if they are worried, the student answers that they are 'fine'. If you think your child is not fine, but does not know how to answer, you could ask what they think *other* Leaving Cert. students will be worrying about tonight. Often this is the ideal way to understand what your own child's worries are.
- Parents can then comment on the worries or those 'other students' in a way that may reassure their own child. For example, a parent might say 'do they really think they will disappoint their parents? Sure parents know that any exam can go wrong, parents only worry if their child will be disappointed'.

- The night before the exam *is* a time when the student should come first in the household. Grumpiness, irritability and annoyances should be ignored as signs of anxiety. Brothers and sisters should be encouraged to be as pleasant as possible. Parents should 'hang around' so that the student can wander in and out of their presence for reassurance and be available for a walk or to share a cup of tea or whatever is helpful
- In summary, the night before the exam is a night for calm, for reassurances, for routine, for being both matter-of-fact but sympathetic, attentive, but not so much so that the student gets tense.
- A good-night hug is usually welcomed, even if it is shrugged off.

Exam Mornings – How Can Parents help?

Parents know their own children. They know what approach would be most helpful on the day the exams begin and on the subsequent exam days of the Leaving Cert. They know if the student likes to talk or be silent, wishes to run over notes or not consult them at all, likes to be totally independent or likes to be pampered a little. People deal with exams in their own way. What is important is to allow them to do that.

The following ideas are also offered for consideration:

- It is important that parents are not under stress from their own working lives during the Leaving Cert. exam time. If a parent can schedule their workload it is better to make this a time of minimum pressure for them.
- If a parent can take a day or so off work that is helpful, but not essential. Sometimes parents can organise their hours at work, their shifts or their workload, to be around before or after the exam, especially in the first day or so of exams until a routine is established.
- Before the exams begin ask students what support they would like and what they would *not* like on the first day of the exam and work out the details with them.

- If students are used to fending for themselves in the morning, it might alarm them to have a large, cooked breakfast awaiting them. Shades of execution come to mind.
- Also, it is better for the student not to deviate too much from normal eating patterns or from the normal morning routine. Having said that it can be nice to have a parent ready and waiting with a nice cup of tea and toast or maybe a pastry or a croissant, something to lift the spirits on the first morning.
- Ensure that more than one means of waking up is provided in the house. Setting an extra clock or booking an alarm-clock call can be helpful. Worry about waking on time in the morning is not conducive to sleep the night before, particularly in a tired student who may already have difficulty falling asleep.
- In the unlikely and unfortunate event that the family should, on this one day, sleep it out, then keep calm anyway. Move quickly, calmly and efficiently and don't berate the student, yourself or anyone else for this unusual occurrence. Murphy's Law gets into some households on exam days and only gets worse with panic.
- If facilities are restricted or in demand, give the student first access to the shower. It is nice to provide some special toiletries, invigorating shower gels, body lotions and plenty of clean, fresh towels. This is not the morning for scrambling around with soapy eyes for a facecloth.
- Keep things cheerful at breakfast.
- Ask students how they are feeling but do *not* give false reassurances such as 'don't worry, you'll be fine'. This particular statement features on the top ten of young peoples' most disliked parental statements.
- Instead it might be helpful to say something like 'I'm sure you're feeling a bit tense today, that's to be expected.' Or you might remind students that 'They say its good to be a bit anxious, it gets the brain working'.
- Allied to this, don't tell them to relax. Did you ever know anyone to relax on command?

- The morning of the exam is not the time for speeches about the importance of the Leaving Cert. Speeches about the end of childhood, of secondary school, how the years have flown or how crucial this day is, are not stress reducers.
- Equally radio announcements about the exam may not be helpful because it turns the exam into a significant national event. Whatever tips were available in the media will probably already have been heard or read in the past few weeks.
- Make sure that the student has everything they need for the day. If they have been studying using one of the essential oils that assist memory, remind them to bring it with them or on their sleeve cuff or on cotton wool. If they are taking 'Rescue Remedy' to steady them, ensure they have it packed. A little thing can throw a student on the day. Don't forget practicalities such as money and all the exam paraphernalia.
- Better not to stress students by asking them too many questions on the day about what they want to bring to the exam. Put what you think they may need, a drink, sweets, chewing gum, tissues etc. beside or into their bag and let them know that you have done so.

Travelling to the Exam

- If students are travelling by bus to the exam, make sure, again, that they have bus-fare. Also that they leave in good time. Traffic is so unpredictable that it is better to err on the side of caution, particularly on the first day when a delay would throw the student's confidence entirely.
- Many students appreciate a lift to the exam if they are not within walking distance. If you are driving them, this is not the day to add to the tension by screaming at other drivers, cursing gridlock, overtaking dangerously or by letting your own anxieties seep through. Keep calm no matter what.
- If the student wants to look over notes in the car, if they want to listen to music, to talk, to hear the radio, to be silent,

don't stop them. This is a day to give them first choice of travel activities.

- Organise things so that there is more than enough time to get there and time to spare for any unforeseen delay, road works, a puncture, a traffic diversion. If you are very early the student can sit quietly in the car and revise on arrival at or near the school.
- Some students like to be dropped off within a short walking distance of the school. This has the advantage of some fresh air and exercise for the student, which is always helpful before an exam. Additionally, the student may meet up with a friend or classmate. It can be reassuring to arrive to the school with a pal.
- If they will let you, a huge hug is wonderfully reassuring, but don't shower students with pre-exam kisses or unusual loving messages. Besides, kids know when their parents are behind them and if you've been looking after them all morning you've already given the best message of support.
- Wish them luck and say that you hope they get a chance to do justice to what they know. This is reassuring because it conveys the message that a good student can have a 'bad' exam. It shows realism. This takes the pressure off.
- On exam days for Irish or foreign languages some parents, who have proficiency in these languages, speak to the student in that language. This can get the student into the mind-set of the language. It can be an amusing way of revising on the way to the exam, particularly if the parent uses humour. However, desist if this is not helpful to the student.
- For other subjects it can be helpful, sometimes, to ask questions in a conversational way e.g. 'tell me about Hamlet?'

Good Luck Messages

- On the morning of the first exam, it is nice to give students a good luck card – preferably a funny one. A humorous card lightens the day and helps perspective. Remember if the card and message are too serious this just adds to the student's burden.

- It is not advisable to promise money as reward for results, particularly if an amount is specified for particular grades or points. To study is a privilege and a students' responsibility, not something for which a student should be paid. Indeed, a 1999 review in the *Psychological Bulletin*, of 128 studies on the effects of rewards on a person's motivation, showed that external tangible rewards could even reduce inner motivation.
- This is not to discount the importance of a little surprise generosity, or some small treat, before the exams as recognition of hard work or after the exams for a celebratory night out for students or to purchase something special. It is the payment per subject and subject grade that is the least effective.
- Finally, if there is a family religion or belief system, this is a good day for prayer. Students often like to know that their parents will go to Mass or the mosque, synagogue or Service or to whatever place of worship the family belong, to invoke whatever higher authority they rely on in their lives.

Outside the Exam Hall

Talking to friends outside the exam hall can be encouraging. It reminds students that everyone is a bit scared in their own way. A laugh with friends is a great releaser of anxiety and may help students to gain perspective.

However, sometimes fellow students engage in scaremongering, which increases anxiety. This is not the time for the student to rush to notes to cover a newly discovered 'definite tip'. If the conversation is not productive, it is better to stay away.

Each student needs to decide on his or her own pre-exam psych-up. Just as some athletes go to a quiet corner to focus, some students also prefer to be alone. Others get psyched by the group and need to make that connection before going into the exam hall. It is the student who decides.

Before entering the hall, the necessities of life should be attended to – nerves and three hours work ahead make a loo visit advisable.

If a student feels panicky the old trick of breathing in and out of a brown paper bag for a minute or so is helpful. In any event it is no harm to remind students to take deep breaths and release their breath *very* slowly to calm the racing heart.

Most importantly, reassure them that anxiety is normal and that it will help to energise and focus them and give them energy during the exam.

Finally tell them to get seated early. To watch their classmates and smile at them as they enter or sit down. This kind of pre-exam communication both releases tension and connects a student to others in a reassuring way. However, suggest that once the exam begins they should focus *only* on themselves, the question they are answering and the time available for each question and answer. This is the moment they have been waiting for, the moment the Leaving Cert. begins.

Reflections on the Day

Ironically, the day the exam begins is the beginning of the end of the process. The strain and stress are now almost over. What students know, they know. They must let regrets go and do their best. If they have not done enough, this is not the time for guilt. Instead they may like to think about it this way; that what they have learnt is an important and valuable life lesson.

They will know their talents and their limitations and what they personally need to do if they wish to succeed in examinations in the future. They will know what way they study, how easy or difficult it is for them to do so, their preferred method of learning and remembering and their own personal style of understanding. Regardless of the outcome the year will not have been wasted.

Sitting the Exam

Understanding the Exam

The tragedy of many examinations is not that the student does not know enough, but that the student knows *too* much and does not convey it.

Too many students do not know how to demonstrate the knowledge they have. They may have vast quantities of information, but they do not provide the essential points that demonstrate this. They cannot distinguish the primary points from the peripheral. This is the first principal of exam success or failure. Answer what is asked. Be relevant. Be brief. Be succinct.

This cannot be said too often. Examinations are not just a measure of knowledge, but of the ability to communicate that knowledge in a clear, succinct manner, within the allocated time. The crucial elements in exam success therefore are:

- Answering the questions that have been asked.
- Not answering what has not been asked.
- Answering within the allocated time.
- Answering every question that can be answered.

Examiners are not privy to what students know unless they show them that they know it. They are also not privy to the following:

To what students *wish* they had written.
To what they *meant* to say but didn't.
To what they *would have said* if they had more time.
To what they *would not have said* if they had time to read over their paper.

The challenge of the exam, therefore, is to condense and convey information in three hours. Parents may wish to suggest some of the following to their children:

At the Start of the Exam

- While the papers are being handed out, the student should sit comfortably in the chair, place both feet firmly on the ground and concentrate on feeling their feet touching the ground. The term 'two feet planted firmly on the ground' does not arise without any basis. Concentrating on the feet helps to steady and 'ground' a student and assists focus and concentration.
- Affirming statements can be very helpful. For example, students might tell themselves, 'I can do this' or 'I am confident. I know enough. I'll be fine'. Affirmations can be quite powerful because they stop negative internal dialogues taking over. If affirmative statements are not used, people can unconsciously panic themselves with negative disconfirming inner thoughts such as *'I won't know anything'*, *'I'll be found out'*, *'I'm going to panic'*.

Reading The Paper

- Papers should be turned over and read meticulously. Too often a student misses a whole section because they looked at one side of a paper only. In the stress of exams it can happen.
- People hold different views on whether the student should launch into the question they know best to steady their nerves or whether they should read all the paper. Except in circumstances of exceptional nerves it is probably advisable to read all the exam paper thoroughly. Then read it again. This is because reading the entire paper helps the student to keep all questions in mind. The brain sometimes even organises answers to later questions before the student gets to them.
- There are other advantages to reading the entire paper. It prevents the answer to a later question being given in an earlier question unnecessarily or repetitively. Additionally,

sometimes a student thinks of an important point for another question. This can be jotted down so that it will not be forgotten when the student comes to answer that particular question later on. Furthermore, later questions sometimes provide important cues to earlier answers.

- Students should make sure they understand exactly how many questions they have to answer and the choices and the options available to them.
- It is essential to know which questions are compulsory. Students who have taken time to become acquainted with exam papers prior to the exams will be familiar with what is compulsory and what is optional. This saves time and reduces stress.

Time, Time and Time Again

.
- One of the biggest mistakes students make is not allowing enough time to answer questions. Students need to be ruthless in ensuring that all questions get sufficient time.
- The extra marks that might be gained by running fifteen minutes over on one question will be a fraction of the marks that will be *lost* by not having time to tackle another question. Better to do four adequate questions than two magnificent questions and leave two questions out.
- This is why, at the start of the exam, students need to calculate the time available for each question allowing time at the end to look over the entire paper. They should then divide the time evenly between questions if there are equal marks for questions. Otherwise, they should allocate time on the basis of the 'value' of the question.
- There are no marks for questions not attempted.
- Should the 'terrible' happen and a student miscalculate, then even writing an opening paragraph and providing a list of the principal points and key ideas will provide a surprising number of marks.

Answering the Questions

- Students should read essay titles very carefully and be sure that their answer addresses *every* element in the title. It is often helpful if the student begins an answer by repeating the question asked. The old maxim tell people what you are going to tell them, then tell them, then tell them what you have told them still works well. It means that answers have a beginning, a middle and an end that are connected.
- It is important that students are not thrown by the wording of questions. Sometimes students have studied and prepared an answer to a question and are flummoxed when the question is not given in the precise wording they were expecting. Students can even end up not answering in an area they know best because of this. Calm down, reread the question and it should seem more familiar.
- It is usually advised that students do their best question first. This gives confidence, demonstrates a standard to the examiner and also ensures that the best question is done well and not rushed at the end. Some people advise that the second best question is done first and that the best question is done second when the student has got into the swing of the exam and is likely to provide their best answer.
- Students can prepare their answers by jotting down in single words or 'spidergrams' the main most important points they wish to make. These should be numbered when the student has decided the order in which to make these points. Answering questions is not just about piling a heap of information on the examiner. It is important to prepare an answer that shows why the student chose to provide certain information and not other pieces of information on that topic.
- Having completed one or two good questions, students are advised to plan out the answers to the remaining questions, particularly the last question. This is because it becomes increasingly difficult as the clock ticks on and adrenaline flows to organise the material in a coherent fashion. Having a list of the main points to be made and the order in which

they will be made allows the student to write at enormous speed on those last questions, rather than frantically trying to gather material in a haphazard way at the end.

- It is always advised that students pay attention to the opening paragraphs, the concluding paragraphs and the first sentence in each paragraph in between. Summaries and conclusions are particularly important because they provide a synopsis for the examiner of the points made.

- Sometimes a summary can even include points that were not made en route that should have been made. If time is against the student, a good summary provides an opportunity to make an effective and powerful conclusion. This leaves the examiner with a sense of strength in the student in relation to the topic

Answering What is Asked

- With the best will in the world, examiners cannot give marks to the student who provides elaborate answers to a question not asked. This cannot be said too often. As they write, students should keep in mind the exact meaning of the question asked and the precise points that would answer that question. Unnecessary elaboration, padding and waffle all make the examiner's task more difficult, sending examiners on an exhausting treasure hunt to find the relevant gems of information.

- Remind students that there are important cues to what they are being asked contained in the specific way the question is put. These words are carefully chosen to help students to answer the questions asked.

  - If they are asked for reasons, give reasons,
  - If they are asked to name, don't explain,
  - If they are asked to explain, don't discuss,
  - If they are asked to discuss, then they should not just define.

- Allied to the point above, the precise terminology in exams is very important. Students need to become acquainted with the meaning of the terms such as:

  - Outline, analyse, examine, synopsise,
  - Debate, Discuss, Describe, Define,
  - Distinguish between, Argue for,
  - Give reasons for, Present, Explain.

- Remind students that some questions carry a command, such as 'analyse', 'explain', 'examine'. Some questions are multi-part questions on which as much attention needs to be paid to the *second half* of the question as is paid to the first instruction. Additionally, there are what might be described as provocative questions to which you are invited to respond. Sometimes a famous quotation is provided. This often calls for a more complex answer than the quote suggests.
- Remind students, also, that there is no benefit in writing three pages on a question that carries few marks and on which they have been asked to write *brief* notes.
- It is important that students demonstrate how they arrived at their answers by demonstrating their working. Formulae should always be included. Steps should be provided in order.
- Summaries of experiments in science do not show the examiner that the student is actually capable of conducting the experiment step by step. All diagrams should be labelled. Graphs should be done carefully and both axes need to be described.

Reading Over the Paper

- Students should read over their answers. This can help to jerk the memory to remember further points, to fill in gaps or to provide linking sentences. These linking sentences allow a logical flow to an argument.

- It is useful if students leave plenty of space at the beginning and the end of questions and a line or two between paragraphs. This stops the paper becoming illegible or untidy if, when a student is reading over their paper, they want to insert a new piece of information or a linking sentence between paragraphs.
- The importance of numbering questions, making it absolutely clear what question is being answered, cannot be overemphasised. Headings and subheadings will provide the examiner with a logical map and guide him or her through the students' answers.
- This is the time to put in any missing labels, diagrams or graphs and to name and number them.
- Reading over the paper ensures that all the important details are attended to.

Summary

- In summary, answers should show that the student has understood the question, has the information required, can provide the salient information, is able to take a position on the topic and can demonstrate that position effectively. Legibility of writing and clarity of expression are important, although as discussed in Chapter 9 illegibility is attended to by the advising examiner.
- Waffling irritates examiners who have to wade their way through the excess to find the essential. It wastes time. It obscures the salient points. It does not achieve marks. Less is more and marks are given for quality, not quantity.

The Weeks of The Exam

After the first exam on the first day, students have passed an important hurdle. The months of anticipation are over. The dreaded has begun. It was not as bad as anticipated. Hopefully.

Students often settle into a routine at this stage and it is usual for study to be focused and concentrated and specifically exam orientated. There is not time to worry, only time to study.

Students may study intensely at this stage. They may stay up late at night cramming information through tired eyes into baffled brains. They have to work exhaustively on the days they actually sit an exam. They often return home worried and ruminating on the points they did or did not make, what they forgot, what they remembered but forgot to write down and what they could not remember until after the paper was handed in.

They have to hold their anxiety at bay over the weeks and get on to the next paper. You can help them. Here are some of the ways.

Talking About the Exam

The last thing a young person needs on return home from an exam is the time worn *'Well, how did you get on? Did you do well?'* Better to say *'welcome home, you look exhausted.'* When they are ready they will tell you. At this stage is it better to ask them how they feel, not what they achieved.

Students need help after each exam is over, to learn from it and to let it go. They need to get on to the next exam not ruminate on the last. The student who tells you they made a major time-error does not need their parents' disappointment added to their own regret. Remarks such as; *'How could you?'* *'Did you not time it?'* *'Had you no watch?'* or *'What were you thinking of?'* are not helpful.

Better to reassure the student that mistiming an exam is a life lesson everyone has to learn. The benefit is that they will be on the lookout and will not make that error for the rest of the Leaving Cert. It can be helpful to say. *'That's disappointing for you.'*, *'I'm sure what you wrote in the questions you did was good. I know it's upsetting but we all do that some time, this was your turn.'*

Equally, students often misread a question and then are devastated after the exam to realise that what they answered what was not what was asked. Worse still, they could have done very well on what was required. Although one can perfectly understand the frustration and disappointment a parent has on receipt of this news, criticism will only send the student into the next exam with their confidence shaken further. In this instance remarks such as 'how could you have misread it?' are not helpful. Instead, it may be helpful to say *'I'm sorry that happened, it's upsetting for you'.*

Finally, students may do badly on their favourite subject. This is particularly unsettling and upsetting for students. It is helpful if parents remind them that their expectations might be particularly high because it is their best subject. They might consider if, relative to other people who do not like that particular subject, they would have done well. Also, it is helpful if parents reassure with something like the following. *'I'm sorry you didn't get a chance to show how much you know on that'. 'Well sometimes we expect too much of ourselves on our best subject.',* or *'Most people have a paper that goes wrong on them. That's tough.'* If all else fails a parent can point out that this is a subject about which they know so much that such knowledge is never a waste.

Other Supports

Being warm, cosy and comfortable, and studying in a pleasant tidy space can really help a student to know that they are cherished and cared for at this time.

Suggest that students have a shower on their return home from exams. Tell them to imagine the tension of the exam washing away. It is also refreshing for students before sitting down to the next bout of study.

It can be helpful to tidy the student's room (not disturbing notes laid out) while they are out at an exam so that they return to a pleasant study place.

As each subject, which has been 'contained' in one of the recommended large coloured boxes, is finished, it is advised to physically move that box and contents out of the student's study place. This clears both a physical and mental space. It also allows the student to see the manageability of the remaining boxes. Remember each box is an exam. Soon only a box or two will remain.

Make sure the student has nice things to eat. A bit of comfort food, nourishing but consoling, is good at this time. Coming home to a meal is very reassuring.

If healthy snacks are available this will prevent the student overdosing on sugar. Parents can also make alternatives to tea, coffee and caffeine drinks available.

When students take breaks they should have first choice of TV or other activities for the duration of the exam. This shows that consideration is being given to the work the student has to do, respect for that endeavour, for the student who is attending to it and respect for the educational process itself.

There is a fine balance between treating student's exams seriously and treating them anxiously. Learning to cope with the inevitable highs and lows, the 'brilliant' papers, the papers that went 'wrong' is all part of learning in which parents challenge and support their children.

These parental supports are remembered and appreciated forever.

Notes
1   Related to theories that hormones influence sex differences in spatial abilities. Proposed in Kolb and Whishaw (1996), pages 458-464.

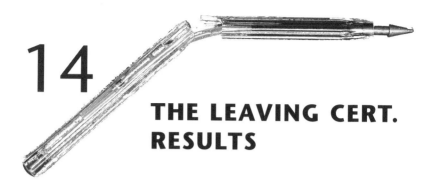

14

THE LEAVING CERT. RESULTS

Information booklets made available by the Department of Education and Science provide insight into the scale of administering, collating, grading and transmitting the results of the Leaving Cert.[1]

There can be as many as sixty thousand students sitting the Leaving Cert. in any one year. More than eight hundred thousand components may be examined. These would include written papers, oral exam, aural assessment and practical work. More than four hundred and thirty-five thousand grades in thirty-one different subjects may be awarded, evaluated by over two thousand eight hundred examiners.

And you wait in trepidation for the only result in the world that matters. Your child's result.

On the day of the results parents wait at work or at home for a phone call, by the door for a glimpse of the result on their child's face, in a car outside the school for a wave of triumph or signal of despair, or by the Internet, to see the magic figures appear on the screen. Wherever parents wait, the day of the results is a tense time.

Students' Emotions Awaiting the Results

If it is tense for the parent, how is the day for the student? The following are some of the feelings young people express:

- Anticipation, excitement and terror.
- Vacillating from a belief that one has done brilliantly to a belief that one has failed totally.
- Some students wondering how to cope with failure in front of their friends.
- Others wondering how to be magnanimous about their good results.
- The students who studied hoping their hard work has paid off.
- The students who didn't trying to remember what they crammed in during those last few days and hoping they may have scraped through.
- The 'points-seekers' terrified that they may miss their coveted place by a small margin.
- The repeats hoping they have pulled it off this time.
- The optimistic, glad it is all over, hopeful, pleased to know the outcome one way or another.
- The students who secretly believe they did much better than anyone would have anticipated, hugging the hope until they can announce their victory.
- There will be many students who will want to thank a favourite teacher for their encouragement and support.
- And some students who want to prove a sceptical teacher wrong in their underestimation of the students' worth.
- There will be students who were ill during the exams feeling cheated that they could not complete them, or compete on equal terms.
- Students who cannot wait to reassure their parents or to make them proud.
- Students terrified of ringing home with bad news, facing their parents with poor results. Students concerned about their parents' emotions. Those who cannot bear to upset or disappoint their parents.
- Students waiting to see the relief and delight on their parents' faces.
- Still other students who know that they themselves can handle disappointment, but who worry that their parents

will be overly and unnecessarily concerned about them if they do not do as well as they had hoped.

- Student who encountered difficult circumstances proud of themselves for sitting the exam at all.
- The students who have a fair idea how they have achieved and who are eager to have it made official and final.
- Finally, there are the students who don't know what to feel or how to feel, who just want to know their results.

Parents' Responses to Results

Parents will want to be particularly supportive towards their children on this day. It is, therefore, important that parents do their own advance anticipation of how they will feel when they hear the results.

They should also think about what they will say, depending on the results their child receives. Parents could consider the following:

- Parents' own experience of school and of exam results. How do they influence the way they will respond to their child's results? Parents need to spend some time considering this seriously. It has far more influence than many people realise.
- The parent who worked hard and succeeded well in exams, without any real help from anyone, will find it hard to relate to the student who, despite every assistance, did not work and achieve.
- The parent who had to struggle through every exam working to exhaustion to achieve, may find it difficult to cope with the student who succeeds brilliantly on apparently little effort.
- The parent who did not have the opportunity to sit the Leaving Cert. may find that they are responding to their emotions about that. These may take the form of tremendous pride, overwhelming joy or maybe even sadness about the opportunities the parent never had.

- Parents also need to examine their expectations of the student's results. Are they realistic? If not, then parents may unwittingly hurt the student who has done their best and who has done well within their capacity.
- What was the relationship during the year with the student? Was it contentious? Did the student reject every offer of parental help? Did the student provide unrealistic reassurance of having everything under control? How does the memory of those interactions influence the parents' response now?
- What response will they now make if their child has done badly? Will they be angry with the child, the school or the system? How will those responses affect their child?
- Did they warn the student repeatedly that study was being left too late, that socialising was too frequent, that commitment was too sparse? Is the parent angry with the student in a way that is hard to hide and bound to leak out? If so, parents may need to vent this anger elsewhere, to each other, by writing it down, to a close and trusted friend, to a close family member. This is *not the time or place* for that anger, however justifiable it may be.
- Will they 'know' if the result is consistent with their child's ability and work throughout school? Will they suggest a re-check? Will they explore other courses and career options? Will they await the CAO offers, or suggest that the student repeat? Each of these responses will play an important part in how the student experiences their results and plans for the next year. Parents, therefore, need to think them out in advance rather than burdening the student with immediate decisions on the day of the results.
- Will the reactions of both parents be similar or different? How will parents respond to the child if they have different responses to the results? Students who experience the approbation of one parent for effort and the disappointment of another parent, who requires brilliance, can feel quite miserable and confused about their results. Have parents had a chance to discuss this, to present a united response to the student?

- How will parents communicate the results to other people in the family and extended family? Parents need to remember that their communications to others will always reach the student at some time in the future.
- Finally, and most importantly, parents need to decide how they will communicate their response to their child in a way that is helpful, supportive and realistic, helping the student to appraise their own efforts and results in a realistic and positive manner.

Getting the Results

Until recent times, most students obtained their results by going to their school. Copies of the provisional results were provided to school and student, one for the school to retain and one for the student to take away. This system also gave the school principal, and any teachers who wished to be present, the opportunity to speak to the students, to congratulate or commiserate and to offer support.

It also ensured that many classmates were on the premises. This was either experienced as helpful or embarrassing or both, depending on the students, their relationship with their peers, the presence or absence of their particular friends and, of course, the results obtained.

Results are now available through the Internet for families with home computers and/or access to the Internet. Students log on to www.examinations.ie and use their PIN (Personal Identification Number) to access their results. Schools may also retain a master list of students' PINs, should a student have any queries in this regard. This provides the opportunity for the student to receive the results alone, in the privacy of the home and to deal with them personally before having to share them with anyone else.

This does not preclude the student from receiving the results through the school in the traditional manner.

Helplines

It is important than any student who is upset or unsure about the implications of their results for Third-Level opportunities can be given the necessary information. Equally, that any student needing clarification has somewhere to turn. For the first week following the issue of results, the Department of Education and Science operates a helpline for schools. This is to allow any initial confusion with regard to the provisional results of individual students to be clarified and resolved.

The National Parents' Council (Post-Primary) also organises an important helpline for students and parents following the issuing of results. This provides information, advice and help to any student or parent who phones. Helpline numbers are usually provided in the national press.

Indeed, much of the information and advice that parents are likely to require in the weeks after the exams will be found in the national press.

This is a useful time to peruse newspaper reports packed with useful discussions about career and course options, lists of PLCs, interviews with colleges and advice about unusual routes into career choices.

There are many instances where direct entry to a course is not possible, but a series of indirect courses or routes can qualify the student for entry to the course at a later date. It can provide the same qualification in the end.

What About the CAO?

Results are also transmitted electronically to the CAO and to UCAS by the Department of Education and Science, so that student places can be processed immediately.

Of course many students will have a good idea of the number of points required for their choices under CAO. They will know, from their Leaving Cert. results, if they are likely to receive a place with a comfortable margin or if they may be borderline and have to endure some further tension and waiting.

The first-round CAO offers follow the Leaving Cert. results.

However, not until the first and second rounds of offers are made and accepted are places final.

Some courses, which are undersubscribed, advertise places in the papers. Keep a look out for these. Sometimes students find adverts for courses they had not previously considered, but which turn out to be eminently suitable to their interests and talents.

The most important message for students of the twenty-first century is that there is something for everyone.

Is There a Mistake?

Given the enormous volume of exams to be evaluated and results to be communicated, it is surprising that so little goes wrong, rather than that mistakes are made. Having said that, what may be a small margin of error statistically can be a traumatic experience personally. For any pupil on whose exam paper an evaluation mistake is made, that error can have serious consequences.

If a student is genuinely amazed by a result then the error factor can be considered. This is because there can be errors in any system. The experience of receiving a mark that is totally different to a student's belief about what they did in the exam does alarm students. Therefore, if the result is totally out of character for the student and the student suffered no specific problem on the day of the exam, then parents can seek a re-check.

It is probably better to do this than to have a student (or parents) torture about the result *ad infinitum*. However, before seeking any re-check students and parents should ask themselves the following:

- Is this grade significant in the overall result?
- What is the likelihood that the grade is wrong?
- If the paper is checked and turns out to be correct how will we feel?
- If the paper is re-checked and the student gets an even lower result, what are the implications of that?

- If the paper is not re-checked, what is the likelihood that in several years time the student may say *'we should have re-checked that mark, I know I did better than that'*. No parent wants the guilt of that.
- The decision to have a re-check ultimately depends on the strength of the belief that a real and significant error was made. The student is the best judge of the likelihood of this, having sat the paper and knowing the extent to which the information to the required number of questions was conveyed and whether or not this was in a comprehensive manner within the time allocated.
- It is important to strike a balance between the benefits of seeking a re-check and the tension and further waiting that this will incur for students and parents.

Finally, applications for appeal of results must be made through the schools. The Department, from whom parents can also seek up-to-date information on the appeals process, usually provides a deadline date for appeals annually. This is usually a date around the end of August or early September. The appeals fee in 2002 is thirty-three Euro *per subject* being appealed.

How Can Parents Help?

Parents usually know intuitively what their child needs. They have their own parenting styles and their own specific insight. They know if their child has succeeded well or has not shown their ability or talent as they might have. They know how to respond to the results, what is fair, what is unfair, what is useful, what would be damaging to the confidence and self-esteem of the teenager. They know how to celebrate and how to commiserate.

In short, parents should tap in to their own, intuitive knowledge of their child at this time, a time for congratulations, reassurances or re-evaluations.

The following may also be helpful:

- If the student has done well, then of course it is important that parents celebrate their child's success. Generous praise has never been found to harm anyone and some third-level motivation can arise from the warmth of the reinforcement students received for the Leaving Cert. results.
- If the child has not achieved well, then empathy is important. Parents need to examine the meaning of this result for the student and what action the student now wishes to take.
- This is also the time that parents send out the message that their love does not depend on their child's success or achievement.
- Once again, it is a time to show the student that there are many options and that there are almost always solutions to what seem to be overwhelming problems.
- It is a time to be creative about choices for the future. A time to look to the future rather than back at the past. What's done is done, but new decisions can be made arising out of what parents and students learn from the exam results.
- It is a time to emphasise the important values in life. Parents who are fortunate enough to have a reasonably responsible, ethical and kind young adult for a son or daughter will retain perspective about the exam results. It is no harm to remind such a child how much these qualities are valued by the parent.

Finally, the way that either celebration or set-back are managed by parents will provide an important lesson for the young person for many years after the Leaving Cert. results may have become a dim memory.

Notes

1 Department of Education Information in this chapter has either been sourced electronically, obtained through Departmental Publications or by telephone directly from the Department offices in Dublin, Athlone and Galway. The kind assistance of Department staff is gratefully acknowledged.

15

THE 'IBIZA SYNDROME'

You would imagine that worries about Leaving Cert. Students should cease when the examination itself comes to an end. That parents would recollect in tranquility the months spent fretting about study. It's over, after all. Hostilities have ended. No more irritability and anger from an over-stressed student or the parents of an under-committed examinee. The battles fought to have the summer months used productively are all in the past, along with the expense of courses and grinds, revision books and notes and weekend immersions in a foreign language.

Just a short year ago, the Leaving Cert. lay ahead with its question mark of survival. Now what's done is done and everyone has survived. Parents did what was required; encouraged, supported, loved, admonished and assisted their children through the grand finale of their school lives.

Time now for holidays, rest, relaxation and resumption of normal family life.

Not so. For many families this is only the beginning of another battle and most worrying event. There are parents who will be amazed to learn that a significant number of students plan post-Leaving Cert., sun-soaked celebrations in foreign parts, the mention of which is dreaded and feared by their parents.

While this condition was originally a Dublin phenomenon, there are rumours that the contagion has spread to other cities and towns in Ireland. Additionally, sightings of Irish students from all parts of the island have been reported in foreign places. This contagious condition, variously known as the *Ibiza Blitz, Magaluf Madness* or the *Aya Napa Syndrome,* is growing.

Regardless of the name, the condition is clear. It is the cathartic carousing, the carrying-on in foreign holiday resorts teeming with hormonally alert, hyperactive, hysterically relieved post-Leaving Cert. revellers that strikes fear into the hearts of already exhausted parents.

Such parental worries are not without substance. Reports, even evidence, of the dangers of these post-Leaving Cert. holidays have been brought back home to the dismay and horror of many parents. Television representations of fun in Fungerola, sex in Ibiza, treats in Aya Napa have not been reassuring to the parents of teenagers. Images of young people, drunk, drugged and clearly unable to determine the risk to their physical safety, their future health and their psychological well-being, obviously add to parental alarm.

And herein lies the problem. There is such predictable divergence between what the young person believes they are requesting and what parents perceive they are condoning, that until each understands the other's position, an amicable solution cannot be reached.

Students' Points

Students do not understand why on earth parents would object to reward for work. Here are their points:

- A holiday in the sun, a nice pool and a few friends for company is not unreasonable after intense study and exams.
- Parents don't even have to pay for it in many instances. Young people protest that if they are prepared to pay for their own holiday from work earnings, then surely they have the right to choose how to spend their own hard-earned money.

- When will their parents trust them? When will they finally let them grow up? If putting in a solid year's study and managing to cope with the final school exam is not a sign of maturity, what else is required?
- Parents are too influenced by media reports. Just because cameras zoom in on the worst images of Iberian imbecility, especially edited to depict the depraved, does not mean that is what they what will happen to them. Many young people feel angry that their parents have bought into media-generated negative ascriptions and descriptions of them.
- It's discriminatory. Post-Leaving Cert. young women feel particularly aggrieved that there is often gender discrimination in operation. The sons can go, they're safe. The daughters are in danger.
- The world is different, travel is different, there are mobile phones, e-mails, and it takes longer to get from Belfast to Bundoran than to Ibiza and back.
- It is not their parents' decision. It's neither illegal nor immoral to take a package holiday to the sun. The problem is parental paranoia.
- A good long summer break is needed before the hard work of college ahead.

Parents' Points

From the parents' perspective, of course they want their children to celebrate and have a nice break, after all the stress of the last year. They agree that students who have worked in summer jobs have the right to spend their own money in their own way. But parents say that they have rights too, especially the right to advise and to deter their offspring from situations of potential physical, psychological, emotional or social harm.

As responsible parents they have the wish to know that their child is safe, where the proposed summer holiday will take place and with whom. Parents would assert these wishes particularly when their child is still under the age of eighteen and cite many reasons for their concerns, including the following:

- Despite the age and maturity of the Leaving Cert. graduates, they may have insufficient experience of the world and insufficient maturity to know all the risks of these holidays.
- *'This is our job'*, parents argue, *'to do what we believe is best'*. The parental role is to be appropriately protective. Everything they have seen of the abysses of debauchery depicted in media reports of certain foreign holiday locations suggests that these are not safe places for young people on their own.
- The issue is not one of trust or distrust of the young person. It is distrust of *other* people, other influences, other mores and the false sense of invulnerability that young people often display at the height of their exuberance, which can have dangerous consequences.
- Parents agree that problems can occur in any situation and in any part of the world, but the risks, they say, are greater if there are too many young people celebrating together and all that that entails.
- The biggest worry is alcohol abuse, particularly reported holiday alcohol patterns. This is because most parents are aware of the connection between alcohol intake and accidents. If the risk of accident multiplies with each small ingestion of drink and by multiples of forty at six alcohol units, then is it any wonder that parents worry? They certainly have reason to.
- The combination of alcohol levels and the risk-taking dispositions of the young, coupled with the total freedom from any concerned adult observers invites images of an array of accidents, motorbikes careering down narrow roads, young people falling over balconies, down lift shafts or off cliffs, car crashes, boating accidents and swimming tragedies.
- It is much more difficult to judge whether or not you are in a safe or a dangerous location when in an unfamiliar country

and culture. Equally, judgments and perceptions of people are altered by the language and cultural differences, so people may be much less wary about whom they go out with, get into a car with or visit. This puts young people at a double disadvantage. They are identifiable to others and these others are not identifiable to them.

- There have been indisputable reports of a number of significant attacks on tourists abroad and descriptions of situations where young men and women have been targeted for assault.
- Date-rape drugs and funny drinks should be considered. Not even the most mature person can avoid being duped if someone is out to do so.
- Finally, parents protest that their worries and fears are, as always, expressions of their love and concern for their children, not attempts to spoil their summer.

As in many conflicts between two seemingly reasonable positions, an impasse is reached. Tragically, this impasse may be terminated with the dreaded words,

'I'm 18, I'm an adult you can't stop me', followed by the even more damaging phrase *'If you go you needn't come back to this house'*.

Now that's no way to end the Leaving. Not with another kind of 'leaving', an unnecessary departure, sadness for both parents and teenagers.

What Can Parents Do?

Well some parents plan well in advance to provide diversionary activities and interests. The possibilities are as endless as parental creativity. Some enrol students in health farms to recover from the exams, with beauty or bodybuilding treats for good measure. Others provide driving lessons throughout the summer instead of a holiday. Some do organise a holiday, but a safe one, with a collection of friends. What could be more beautiful than parts of Ireland to revive the soul and heal the weary spirit of the student?

The possibilities are endless, depending on the interests and hobbies of the student. Alternatively parents can ask the 'graduate', what their plans for the summer months are and be ready with a range of alternatives if the dreaded *'I was thinking of Ibiza'* is voiced.

This is the time to say, *'What a shame, I thought you would like to learn to drive, this summer'* or *'Pity, so and so is advertising an incredible job as film extras'*, or *'So you don't mind missing the ...'* (here parents would mention whatever the interested young person would love, a course in Art, work on an archaeological dig, a job on a cruise ship, lessons learning a musical instrument, the chance to earn good money at a summer job or simply the opportunity to chill out for a while after the past year). This is not manipulation. It is providing alternatives – work experience, relaxation or summer work – and inviting the young person to consider them.

But if a decision about going abroad *has* to be made the following may be considered:

- Before making a firm decision about the holiday, seek and listen carefully to *all* the details from the young person about the proposed event. There is no point in ranting to them about the terrors of Torremolinos if they are off to Trieste. Let them know that you are not just dismissing their wish to go away out of hand, but that you genuinely want to know about all about it.
- Having said that, find out exactly where they want to go, with whom, for how long and to do what? There are some young people who go away together just for a rest and companionship. Is the holiday with a few close friends or a large gang? The larger the group the higher the statistical risk of problems arising.
- Explain that your only concern is for their safety, in the situation. That is not a reflection on their capacity to make good judgments or to behave maturely.

- Acknowledge that it is possible to have a genuine sun-soaked holiday without the alarming trimmings and that as parents you simply require the reassurance of detailed information.
- An important 'detail' is who else is going. Be sure that you know the friends that are going away with them and that you have some trust in these accompanying friends? If this is the first time you have heard them mentioned and you have never met them, be suspicious. Why have they just appeared?
- The choice of resort is important, the kind of activities on-site, the age-range of the other holiday makers in the complex. What travel agents are they planning to go with?
- Some parents seek reassurance by checking safety aspects with travel agents or the holiday complex directly. Parent and child can get this information together from the Internet, making the exercise a cooperative rather than a contentious one. Typical queries include information on medical facilities, crime rates against tourists, on-site security and whether or not there is a twenty-four hour reception. It is also useful to know the location of travel agents local office vis-à-vis the resort and have all the information possible about what is covered by insurance and details about nearby resorts and the activities they provide.
- Some parents supplement their children's budget by providing expensive accommodation. This increases the likelihood of their children being in the company of an older more staid generation, in a twenty-four hour reception area with more vigilant staff, security and fellow holidaymakers.
- Many parents rightly base their view on their unique knowledge of their own child. Ask yourself how mature and responsible your child has been in other situations. Do you trust that on a night out they will not drink too much? Have they taken drugs? Did you ever find them drunk? Have they come home on time and respected other family rules in the past? Have they demonstrated maturity in other areas? The level of maturity and responsibility of the young person is an important factor in determining how they will respond in a new situation.

- Always remind young people that your concern is out of love, and *not* distrust or a wish to spoil their fun. That you trust them, but not all those people around them or the world they live in. Remind them of your responsibility as parents not to expose them to more challenges to their maturity than they are able to handle.
- Ask them to consider how they would feel if you were going into a situation that terrified them, but which you thought was quite safe? What would they need to know from you to be reassured that you would be safe? Invite them to consider what concerns they would have if they were in the parental role.
- Finally, if this really is not right for your particular child do not be afraid to say 'no' and to express why you are worried. If they are under eighteen you have a specific right to do so. But if, because of their age, adult status and determination there is little you can do bar physically incarcerating them, avoid the dire threats of expulsion of them from the family. Remaining, despite all, in good relationship with young people is their greatest protection and parents' most challenging job.

Points for Young People

Young people do need to be reminded how much adults respect them and know that this is their special time and that if they can they should enjoy their youth, energy, and enthusiasm. They deserve a break, they are only young once and summer stretches ahead. Finally free from worry and exams what is the harm in a holiday? Why are people so against it? It may be helpful to invite them to consider the following:

- First make sure that what you are choosing to do is really safe for you. There have been many young people who bitterly regretted going on the post-Leaving holiday and who were so overwhelmed by the gang that they were miserable just trying to keep themselves safe at discos and on nights-out.

- Remember that there are situations in which friends get lost or abandon you to find your own way home, alone in risky situations.
- There are accounts of young men being beaten up, injured and having their money stolen. Of course, it can happen anywhere in the world, including at home, but the experience is different at home where there are familiar people, services and hospital systems.
- Remember that what sometimes looks like fun can be better in the anticipation and the 'telling' than in the actual event.
- If the holiday is safe, reassure your parents about it. Give them information. Usually parents are not prying or interfering or disrespecting your young adulthood. They just want to know that you are safe. Don't be offended by their questions. We only worry about those we love.
- Tell them exactly who will be there, where you will stay, how they can contact you and when you will contact them. Mobile text will let them know that you have arrived safely and the promise of a quick daily text saying *alive and fine* will reassure them. If it is a safe holiday you will not mind if they have all the details. If it's not, do you really want to go?
- Consider the advice they have given you in the past. Has it been good? If you are alive, safe, without injury or major trauma having happened in your life so far, maybe they have been appropriately protective of you so far? Do you think you should listen to them more carefully about this?
- If your parents are totally opposed to it, ask yourself if this is the ideal way to celebrate the end of school life. Could you have as much fun in some other way without all the hassle and worry? Will it strain relationships on your return?
- What are the risks? Are you really ready for this if it goes wrong?

Leaving Ibiza

At the end of the day, each family is unique and parents and children will find their own solutions to this new phenomenon. It is worth remembering that clinical work inevitably shows that young people do appreciate parents who are concerned enough about them to draw boundaries; to say 'I cannot let you do this because it may not be safe'.

Deep down there is an appreciation for parents who set a time, a deadline, a limit to activities, who care enough to fight with or for their child's safety. Even if it is not often acknowledged, even if it is often only to be conceded many years later in retrospect, appreciation for true parental concern is high.

The saddest young people are usually those whose parents let them do exactly what they like. A reminder of this may inform the holiday debate.

After all, there is nothing more hurtful than indifference and the intensity of battles between children and parents is often a mirror of the intensity of their love.

16

LOOKING BACK,
LOOKING FORWARD

Although the focus of this book has been on the Leaving Cert. year, that is but the final lap in a long, educational journey. The Leaving Cert. is the culmination of twelve or more years of attending school with a wealth of memories accumulated over those years.

The journey from infancy to adulthood co-occurs with the journey from Junior Infants to Leaving Cert. Children do their growing and their learning in tandem.

At each juncture along the way parents will have tried to maintain a balance in their support. Too much help is non-productive. Too little help would expose students to challenges beyond their capacity. Without any help they could lose confidence and give up. This is a yet another delicate and difficult parental balance, which will have been negotiated during the past year, particularly pertinent because the Leaving Cert. student is also a young adult.

Parents are conscious at this Leaving Cert. stage that their role is not to do the exam for the student, but to support the student who is doing the exam. They know that too much help denies students the dignity of their own decisions about study, opportunities for learning and choices for the future, making choices and coping with the consequences of those choices. They must learn to succeed and they must learn to fail. Life skills must be developed in the course of the Leaving Cert. because those skills will be needed going into the future.

Parents will also have discovered that supporting students is not about removing their responsibility, relieving them of challenges or denying their difficulties. They will have discovered that the 'learning' that takes place in the Leaving Cert. year extends well beyond academic achievement. They will have discovered that, regardless of examination results, the process of doing the Leaving Cert. may have provided many learning opportunities for their children.

This is important in educational terms. Learning is a dialectical process whereby a child learns through problem-solving experiences shared with someone else. In early childhood the parent takes most responsibility in parent-child interactions. By college the responsibility should have shifted to the student. Parents, by this stage, will have provided what Vygotskians[1] call *scaffolding* for learning. This means that parents adjust their help and intervention at each stage, encouraging, challenging, allowing experimentation providing apprenticeship and instilling in the young person the necessary skills for future problem solving.

The student who enters college will have to know how to engage in learning in this dialectical way. This means being independent in some tasks but being able to seek help for others. Reaching adulthood successfully is not just about achieving independence[2] but about negotiating interdependence[3]. That is, knowing when to ask for help and knowing when to stand alone. This is the life stage when parents and child must renegotiate their relative responsibilities.

The learning opportunities inherent in the Leaving Cert. may have included the following:

- Some students may have finally recognised their talents. They may have discovered that they could complete the year with confidence in their abilities.
- They may have achieved well and have learned the ingredients of achievement for them. They may have communicated appropriately with their parents as resources in their endeavours.

- Some students may have identified specific difficulties that they need to work on or get help with.
- There are students who will have found unexpected psychological resources within themselves, strengths they had not previously known that they possessed, like the strength to encounter setbacks, yet continue despite them.
- They may have learned to motivate themselves, not just when terror set in, but in a sustained way throughout the year.
- Students may have found strategies to self-start their study session each evening. This is a major accomplishment and a student who has found the means to apply him or herself to study has acquired an important skill.
- Some students will have learned, with the help of their parents, how to manage their time and organise their learning. This is an important pattern that will stand to them throughout their lives.
- Other students may have learned how impossible it is to achieve any goal without a plan and adherence to it.
- Some students may have increased their sense of identity as being able to survive under stress. Others may have learned that, for them, stressful situations are to be avoided where possible.
- Sadly there may be students who will have learned about coping despite significant loss and grief. They will have taken the significant step into the experience of mourning. Their perspective on life may have changed as a result.
- There may be students who have had to cope with family difficulties.
- Other students will have had to overcome or adapt to educational or learning disadvantages.
- There will be students who may have been physically or mentally unwell and students who may have been depressed, panicked or distressed. How that was dealt with will have significant impact for the rest of their lives.
- Then there are students who may have learned *how* to ask for help, *when* to ask for help and when they had to help themselves, because the task was theirs' alone.

- This balance of assuming responsibility for themselves, while being able to seek the support of others, is an important lesson for students. It is a particularly important lesson to learn before moving into third level.

Finally, while students who are overly dependent on parental structures and supports do sometimes achieve high points at Leaving Cert. level, they often find themselves ill-equipped for the third-level regime, which relies primarily on students themselves to plan and monitor their own study.

This will be their next task and their next lesson: how to cope with the new structures in third level.

Going into the Future

Parents are understandably delighted when their children achieve the points in the Leaving Cert. that allow them to pursue the courses of their choice. For many young people this is the beginning of the best time of their lives, their student days, the culmination of the school process and the privilege of education as young adults.

However, the delight of this year can change into the disappointment of next year for some students if they do not have the skills to survive in third level. Some of these skills need to be acquired in the Leaving Cert. year. Time-management is a particular example and the student who has learned this throughout the year has obtained an important skill for third-level life (or indeed for further training, apprenticeship or the world of work). Other skills will need to be acquired in the year ahead.

Students who are going into college need to be absolutely clear about what they want to do, exactly what the course they have signed up for entails and that they have a genuine interest in the course. Most importantly, students need to be very sure that the course was not chosen because it fell within the expected points capacity of the student. This is often the source of disappointment and dropout for students.

What the Research on Third Level Says

The pattern of non-completion amongst first year students at third level has been a cause of considerable concern for some years. Research[4] has revealed how ill-prepared many students are for this next phase and how ill-equipped many third-level institutions are to help them.

One of the most important and meticulous studies of non-completion was a study in three Institutes of Technology in 1999[5], which examined patterns of non-completion amongst first year students. This study compared the experiences of those who did not complete with those who did. This was based on data from CAO records and a survey of 1,526 first year students.

In this study the most significant social and personal factors that emerged were the following:

- Unclear career aspirations.
- Lack of guidance when making career choices.
- Level of prior academic achievement.
- Difficulty with the academic demands of the course.
- Financial difficulties.
- Working part-time.
- Lack of preparation for third level.

It is particularly significant that many students started courses and then found that they had neither the interest nor the aptitude for them. Others were disappointed in the courses because what they expected to learn was not what was being provided.

Additionally, the many demands of the transition from school to college exceeded the capacity of some students to cope. For some students this involved the following:

- Moving to a new location.
- Undertaking a new course of study.
- Having to organise accommodation.

- Engaging in total self-care.
- Making new friends.
- Integrating into the system.

These tasks require more skills and adjustment than many students are capable of without significant supports.

What Should a Parent Do?
- Psychological preparation is the first stop. Students should ask themselves why they choose the college they chose. Was it for convenience, close by, on a bus route, because friends were going there or because the course they wanted to do most is provided by the college?
- Secondly students need to be very sure about their actual choice of course. They should not take courses that they do not have a genuine interest in and/or aptitude for. This applies particularly to students who may not have got their first choices on CAO and who 'settle' for a later and much less desired option. This may be a mistake and a disappointment, and may erode the student's confidence.
- All students should acquaint themselves with exactly what the course they are to enter entails. The 1999 research by Healy, Carpenter and Lynch cited above shows the need for colleges to provide more precise information specifying the demands of courses rather than abstract descriptions. Students need to know how many lectures, for how many hours, on how many days per week they must attend. They need to know exactly the areas they will be studying, the number of assignments that will be required of them and any other demands of the course that the student may not have anticipated when undertaking to do it.
- Students also need to ask themselves the following questions: *Why did I choose this course? Who thought it was a good choice for me? Why? Who didn't think I should do this course? Why? What decided me to go ahead with it? What do I know about it? What am I looking forward to in it? What am I worried about? Do I know anyone who is currently doing the same*

course? What does that person think about it? What advice could they give me?

- It here is one particular primary textbook that is recommended it can be worthwhile to invest in it or borrow it from the library and scrutinise it. The primary recommended textbooks tend to have an overview of the general course areas. This provides valuable insight into the kind of material the student will be learning.
- When students get a flavour of what they may be learning it can do two things. Firstly it can increase their confidence about the year ahead. Secondly, it can alert the student who may have made the wrong choice. They can then go and find out more about the course if they are uncertain and review their choice if necessary. Better to learn at this stage than a few weeks into college.
- Just as in the summer before Leaving Cert, so too in the summer before college, there are advantages to doing some preliminary reading. For example, a student who is going to study philosophy might consider reading some introductions to philosophy or the ideas of significant thinkers. The student to whom that seems like an enormous chore might consider whether or not they are likely to be engaged by philosophical ideas at third level.
- Students who have had past academic struggles need to be alert to the academic demands of third level and to the possibility that increased academic demands may be a difficulty for them. They need to be prepared to get whatever academic support they require early in the college year, before the course overwhelms them.
- There are very practical financial considerations that should be decided upon in the summer months. Parents and students may need to work out in advance the degree of financial strain the course will impose on the student and on the family. In the light of the research showing that those students who were financially burdened were less likely to complete first year, this is an important consideration.

- Finances are a particular consideration if a student is studying away from home because of the extent of the financial imposition this can be on parents. The details of budget need to be worked out, otherwise some students are out of pocket after a week on a monthly allowance. This is the time to decide how much and in what way the student will be financed. Also how frequently the student will return home (to be fed and with the bag of washing!!) and the practicalities of frequent visits depending on the location of the college.
- Finding accommodation that is suitable is very important. Obviously summer is the time to investigate this thoroughly. But before even doing so students and parents need to work out what is affordable and what is most conducive to study.
- Decisions need to be made about whether the student should be in bed-sit, apartment or house. Different accommodation suits different students. There are those who would be lonely on their own but highly distracted if sharing with overly lively less conscientious students in a house.
- Parents also need to ask themselves a number of questions. How responsible is the student? How capable of cooking, cleaning, looking after him or herself? How has this person managed before living with others e.g. sharing at boarding school or Irish College or in other contexts? Would the student become lonely or disheartened so that being with other people is important? Would the student be irritated by the noise and activities of living with others, so that more individual accommodation would work best? What about digs? Digs is often recommended for first year students living away from home because it can combine the support of living with a family but the independence of being away from family. There is someone to mind and monitor at some level in this situation.
- There are other less concrete practical and psychological factors that may need attention. For example, what is the experience for the student and for the family if the student

is the first family member to attend college? Students can sometimes feel cut off from their family if they are away from home, and families may feel that their child has little time for them in the activities of college life. These potential emotions need to be worked out in advance of college attendance.[6]

Finally, the past Leaving Cert. year will have provided parents with some insight into the student's capacity to manage their time and their study and to balance work and play. Students who were overly dependent on parental help in many aspects of self-care from budgeting money to budgeting time will need to consider the demands of total self-management that arise in student life away from home.

What Will Be Remembered After the Leaving Cert.?

Just as the first day at school remains a strong childhood memory, so too, the last day at school is a memory many people retain for the rest of their lives.

It is high amongst the significant events in school life. People leave school with a store of remembrances. They remember special teachers, a picture on a classroom wall or a name scratched on a desk. They may remember the warmth of a teacher's praise, the cold chill of critique, the pain of effort and the thrill of understanding. They may recall the images of a poem, the colours in a sentence, the smell of school corridors, the light shining though a classroom window, or the window promising a world beyond it.

Most parents will remember all of the steps their children took on the educational road. A series of vivid images: the slow progress of a squirming pencil across the page, the first words read thumb by thumb from a book, the answer to a sum, the chanting of 'tables', the new school uniform of secondary school, the first exam, this last exam – the Leaving Cert.

And as they remember the past, parents would want their children to know that they did what they could to help them over the years, particularly in that final Leaving Cert. year. They would hope that their children would recall the support, understanding, praise and encouragement they received. That they would remember how they were helped in their studies, but more importantly, how they were supported when they could not study at all. How they were challenged to be independent, to self-manage, to time-manage and to self-discipline, yet how they were guided gently when help was needed in these tasks. They would hope that their children were always reassured that they had talents. That this confidence in themselves helped them to create, or find, their niche in life. That points were kept in perspective and that perspective was maintained on the entire process.

Parents would want their children to recall that they were loved and valued for the young people they were and not just for their capacity to achieve. And that in years to come, when their children could no longer remember their exam results, they would nonetheless remember the many lessons they learned throughout the Leaving Cert. year. And they would remember the parents who provided some of these lessons.

Finally, parents may hope that their children will remember that this was the year they learned that the most important personal accomplishments in life are rarely ones that can be measured.

That would be leaving 'The Leaving' with something important for life.

Notes

1   The interested reader may wish to study some of the writings of Lev
    Vygotsky, whose views of cognitive development warrant a revisit.
2   See the writings of Erik Erikson on identity and on the adolescent's
    quest for independence.
3   Chickering, A., Reisser, L. (1993) *Education and Identity.* Jossey-Bass,
    San Francisco.
4   Healy, M., Carpenter, A., & Lynch, K (1999) *Non-Completion in
    Higher Education: A study of First year Students in Three Institutes of
    Technology.* Also Morgan, M., Flanagan, R., Kellachan, T. (2001) *A
    Study of Non-completion in Undergraduate University Courses,* Dublin,
    HEA.
5   Healy et al (1999), cited above.
6   Carpenter, A. (1996) *The First Year Student Experience: Proceedings of
    Conference of CSSI,* Derry, Northern Ireland.

REFERENCES AND USEFUL READING

Abramsom, L.Y., Metalsky, G.I. & Alloy, L.B., (1989) 'Helplessness Depression: A theory based subtype of depression.' *Psychological Review* 96, 358-372.

Altheide, D. L., & Johnson, J. M., (1994) 'Criteria for Assessing Interpretive Validity in Qualitative Research', in Denzin, N.K. & Lincoln, Y.S., (eds.) (1994) *Handbook of Qualitative Research* Sage, London. 485-499.

Anderson, H., (1997) *Conversation, Language and Possibilities: A Post-Modern Approach to Therapy.* Basic Books, New York.

Andrews, P., (1994) 'Adolescent Breakdown', in Keane, C., (ed.) *Nervous Breakdown.* RTÉ / Mercier Press, Cork. 137-147.

Andrews, P., (1995) 'The Adolescent in Psychotherapy', *Irish Journal of Child and Adolescent Psychotherapy* 1 (1) 47-53.

Archer, S.L, (ed.) *Interventions for Adolescents' Identity Development.* Sage, Newbury Park CA.

Arnett, J.J., (1999) 'Adolescent Storm and Stress Reconsidered', *American Psychologist* 1999, 54, 5 317-326.

Baird, A.A., Gruber, S.A., Cohen, B.M., Renshaw, P.F., Steingard, R.J., Yurgelin-Todd, D.A. (1999) 'FMRI of the amydala in children and adolescents', *Journal America, Acad. Child and Adolescent Psychiatry* 1999; 38(2) 195-199.

Barry, J., (1993) 'Alcohol use in post-primary school children', *Irish Medical Journal*, 86 (4):128-129.

Bates, A., (1994) 'Depression', in Keane, C., (ed.) *Nervous Breakdown*. RTÉ/Mercier Press, Cork. 27-36.

Bates, T., (1999) *Depression: The Common Sense Approach*. Newleaf, Gill and Macmillan, Dublin.

Battle, J., (1979) 'Self-Esteem of Students in Regular and Special Classes', *Psychological Reports* 42, 745-746.

Battle, J., (1992) *Culture-Free Self-Esteem Inventories*. (Examiners Manual) Pro. Ed. Texas. (First published 1981).

Beck, A.T., Rush, A.J., Shaw, B.F., Emery, G., (1979) *Cognitive Therapy of Depression*, Guilford, New York.

Beck, A. T., Emery, G., & Greenberg, L., (1985) *Anxiety disorders and phobias: A cognitive perspective*. Basic Books, New York.

Beitchman, J.H., Wilson, B., Brownlie, E.B., Walters, H., Lancee, W., (1996) 'Longterm consistency in speech/language profiles; Developmental and academic outcomes', *Journal of the American Academy of Child and Adolescent Psychiatry*, 35. 1-11.

Beitchman, J.H., & Young, A. R., (1997) 'Learning Disorders With a Special Emphasis on Reading Disorders: A Review of the Past 10 Years', *Journal of the American Academy of Child and Adolescent Psychiatry*, 36. 8. 1020-1032 [special article].

Bernardes, J., (1993) 'Responsibility in Studying Postmodern Families', *Journal of Family Issues* 14: March. 35-49.

Blonder, L.X., Bowers, D., & Heilman, K.M., (1991) 'The role of the right hemisphere on emotional communication', *Brain* 114. 1115-1127.

Booth, R., (1994) 'Panic', in Keane, C (ed.) *Nervous Breakdown*. RTÉ / Mercier Press, Cork. 93-101.

Boyne, E., (ed.) (1993) *Psychotherapy in Ireland*. Columba Press, Dublin.

Brady, T., (1994) 'Bereavement: When the Abnormal may be Normal', in Keane, C., (ed.) *Nervous Breakdown*. RTÉ / Mercier Press, Cork. 159-171.

Burr, V., (1995) *An Introduction to Social Constructionism*. Routledge, London.

Buzan, T., (1974) *Use Your Head!* BBC Publications, London.

Buzan, T., (2001) *Headstrong: How to Get Physically and Mentally Fit*. Thorsons, London.

Campbell, D., (1999) 'Family Therapy and Beyond: Where is the Milan Systemic Approach today?', *Child Psychology and Psychiatry Review* 4, 2:76-84.

Campbell, D.G., (2000) *The Mozart Effect for Children: Awakening Your Child's Mind, Health and Creativity with Music*. William Morrow & Co.

Carpenter, A., (1996) 'The First Year Student Experience': *Proceedings from Conference of CSSI*. Derry.

Carpenter, A., (1997) 'A Systemic analysis of non-completion in Higher Education'. *Proceedings from 5th European Congress of Psychology*. Dublin.

Carr, A., (2000a) *Evidence Based Practice with Children and Adolescents: A critical review of psychological interventions with Children, Adolescents and their families*. Routledge, London

Carr, A., (2000b) *Family Therapy Concepts, Process and Practice*. Wiley, Chichester

Carroll, D. (1984) *Biofeedback in Practice*. Longman, New York.

Carskadon, M.A. Acebo, C., Richardson, G.S. & Tate, B.A., (1997) 'An approach to studying circadian rhythms of adolescent humans', *Journal of Biological Rhythms* 12, 3, 278-289.

Caulfield, M.B., Fischel, J.F., DeBaryshe, B.D., & Whitehurst, G.J., (1989) Behaviour Correlates of Developmental Expressive Language Disorder', *Journal of Abnormal Child Psychology*, Vol. 17. No. 2. 187-201.

Chambers, E., & Northedge, A., (1998) *The Arts Good Study Guide* Open University Press. Milton Keynes.

Cheale, D., (1993) Unity and Difference in Postmodern Families. *Family Issues* Vol. 14 - 5-19.

Chickering, A., Reisser, L. (1993) *Education and Identity*, Jossey-Bass, San Francisco.

Clifford, M. (2002) 'Free Education? Only to those who can afford it' *Sunday Tribune*, August 4, 2002, p.17

Cohen, N.J., Davine, M., & Meloche-Kelly, M., (1989) Prevalence of Unsuspected Language Disorders in A Child Psychiatric Population. *Journal of the American Academy of Child and Adolescent Psychiatry*, 28. 107-111.

Connolly, J.F., (2001) 'Suicide and The Media', in Foster-Ryan, S. & Monahan, L (eds.), *Echoes of Suicide*. Veritas, Dublin.

Coopersmith, S., (1986) *Self-Esteem Inventories*. Consulting Psychologists Press, Inc. California.

Dabrowski, K., (1972) *Psychoneurosis is not an illness*. Gryf, London.

Dallos, R. & Draper, R., (2000) *An Introduction to Family Therapy*. Open University Press.

Daly, M., (2001) 'School: Minding Those at Risk', in Foster-Ryan, S & Monahan, L (eds.) *Echoes of Suicide*. Veritas, Dublin.

Deem, J., (1993) *Study Skills in Practice*. Houghton Mifflin, Boston.

Delisle J.R., (1990) 'The gifted adolescent at risk. Strategies and resources for suicide prevention among gifted youth', *Journal for the education of the Gifted*, 13. 212-228.

Denzin N.K. & Lincoln, Y.S., (eds.) (1994), *Handbook of Qualitative Research*. Sage, London.

De Roiste (1996) 'Sources of worry and happiness in Ireland'. *The Irish Journal of Psychology*, 1996, 17,3 193-212.

Dowling, E., & Osborne, E., (1999) *The Family and the School: A Joint Systems Approach to Problems with Children*. (second edition) Routledge, London.

Dowling, E, & Gorell Barnes, G., (2000) *Working with Children and Parents through Separation and Divorce*. Macmillan Press, London.

Drudy, S. & Lynch, K., (1993) *Schools and Society in Ireland*. Gill and Macmillan, Dublin.

Ehlers, A., (1995) 'A 1-year prospective study of panic attacks: Clinical course and factors associated with maintenance', *Journal of Abnormal Psychology*, 104. 164-172.

Ellis, C. & Flaherty, M.G., (eds.) (1992) *Investigating Subjectivity: Research on Lived Experience*. Sage, London.

Erikson, E., (1968) *Identity, Youth and Crisis*. Faber, London.

Fitzpatrick, C., Deehan, A., (1999) 'Competencies and Problems of Irish Children and Adolescents', *Irish Journal of Medical Science*, 156. 2 19-221.

Fontana, A., & Frey, J.H., (1994) 'Interviewing: The Art of Science', in Denzin N.K. & Lincoln, Y.S., (eds.) *Handbook of Qualitative Research*. Sage, London. 361-376.

Foster-Ryan, S., (2001:) 'Suicide: Practical Response in The Post-Primary School', in Foster-Ryan, S., & Monahan, L., (eds.) *Echoes of Suicide*. Veritas, Dublin. 129-152

Foster-Ryan, S., & Monahan, L., (eds.) (2001) *Echoes of Suicide*. Veritas, Dublin.

Fowler, R., (1991) *Language in the News: Discourse and Ideology in the Press*. Routledge, London.

Fox, N.J., (1993) *Postmodernism, Sociology and Health.* Open University Press, Buckingham.

Freud, A., (1958) 'Adolescence', *Psychoanalytic Study of The Child*, 13, 255-278.

Fry, R., (1997) *Last Minute Study Tips.* The Career Press, Kogan Page, London.

Gardner, H. (1985) *Frames of Mind: The Theory of Multiple Intelligences.* Basic Books, New York.

Gardner, H. (1993) *Creating Minds.* Basic Books, New York.

Gardner, H., (1999) *Intelligence Reframed: Multiple Intelligences of the 21st Century.* Basic Books, New York.

Gecas, V. & Mortimer, J.T., (1987 :) 'Stability and change in the self-concept from adolescence to adulthood', in Honess, T., & Yardley, K., (eds.) *Self and Identity: Perspectives across the Lifespan.* Routledge & Kegan Paul London. 265-286.

Gergen, K.J. & Davis, K., (eds.) (1985) *The Social Construction of the Person.* Springer-Verlag, New York.

Gergen, K.J., (1991) *The Saturated Self: Dilemmas of Identity in Contemporary Life.* Basic Books, New York.

Gillberg, C., (1995) *Clinical Child Neuropsychiatry.* Cambridge University Press, Cambridge.

Goleman, D., (1996) *Emotional Intelligence: Why It Can Matter More Than IQ.* Bloomsbury, London.

Gotlib, I. H. & Lee, C.M., (1989) 'The social functioning of depressed patients: A longitudinal assessment', *Journal of Social and Clinical psychology*, 8, 223-237.

Gray, C. and Mulhern, G., (1998) 'Age and sex-related differences in automaticity for mental addition', *The Irish Journal of Psychology* 19. 2-3. 386-393.

Grant, A., (2002) 'Identifying Students' Concerns: Taking a Whole Institutional Approach', in Stanley, N. & Manthorpe,

J., (eds.) *Student's Mental Health Needs: Problems and Responses*. Jessica Kingsley Publishers, London. 83-105.

Giedd J.N., Blumenthal J., Jeffries N.O., et al. 'Brain development during childhood and adolescence: a longitudinal MRI study', *Nature Neuroscience*, 1999; 2(10): 861-3.

Gurevitch, M., Bennett, T., Curran, J. & Woollacott, J., (eds.) (1994) *Culture, Society and The Media*. Routledge, London. (First published 1982 by Methuen).

Harré, R., (1995:) 'Discursive Psychology', in Smith, J.A., Harré, R. & Van Langenhove, L., (eds.) *Rethinking Methods in Psychology*, Sage, London. 143-159.

Harrington, R., Whittaker, J. & Shoebridge, P., (1998) 'Psychological Treatment of depression in children and adolescents: A review of treatment research', *British Journal of Psychiatry* 173, 291-298.

Hartley, J., (1994) The Psychology of Successful Study, *The Psychologist*, 7. 459-460.

Hawton, K. Simkin, S., Fagg, J. & Hawkins, M., (1995) 'Suicide in Oxford University Students 1976-1990', *British Journal of Psychiatry* 166, 44-50.

Healy, M., Carpenter, A., & Lynch, K., (1999) 'Non-completion in Higher Education: A Study of First Year Students in Three Institutes of Technology': IT Carlow.

Healy, N. & Murray, M., (2002) 'The role of family therapy in psychiatry' *Irish Psychiatrist* 3. 3. April/May 02.

Henggeler, S., Schoenwald, S., Bordon, C., Rowland, M. & Cunningham, P., (1998) *Multisystemic Treatment of Antisocial Behaviour in Children and Adolescents*. Guildford, New York.

Hetherington, M. & Stanley-Hagan, M., (1999) 'The adjustment of children with divorced parents: a risk and resiliency perspective', *Journal of Child Psychology and Psychiatry*, 40, 129-140.

Hill, P., (1993) 'Recent Advances in Selected Aspects of Adolescent' Development. J.', *Child Psychology and Psychiatry* Vol. 34, 1. 69-99.

Honess, T. & Yardley, K., (eds.) (1987) *Self and Identity: Perspectives across the Lifespan.* Routledge & Kegan Paul, London.

Hornsby, B., (1984) *Overcoming Dyslexia: A straightforward guide for families and teachers.* Martin Dunitz Ltd., London.

Houlihan, B., Fitzgerald, M. & Regan, M., (1994) 'Self Esteem, depression and hostility in Irish adolescents', *Journal of Adolescence* 1994, 17 565-577.

Hynd, G.W. & Semrud-Clikeman, M., (1989) 'Dyslexia & brain morphology' *Psychological Bulletin* 1989 106: 444-482

Jacobson, L., (2002) 'Identifying Students' Mental Health Problems in Primary Care Settings', in Stanley, N. & Manthorpe, J., (eds.) *Student's Mental Health Needs: Problems and Responses.* Jessica Kingsley Publishers, London. 121-143.

James, D., Lawlor, M., (2001) Psychological Problems of Early School Leavers, *Irish Journal of Psych. Med.* 2001; 18(2) 61-65.

Jamison, K.R., (1997) *An Unquiet Mind: A Memoir of Moods and Madness.* Random House, New York.

Jolly, J.B., (1993) 'A multi-method test of the cognitive contentspecificity hypothesis in young adolescents', *Journal of Anxiety Disorders,* 7. 223-233.

Kaufman, A.S., (1994) *Intelligent testing with the WISC-111.* Wiley, New York.

Kelleher, M.J., (1996) *Suicide and The Irish.* Mercier Press, Cork.

Kelly, G.A., (1991) *The Psychology of Personal Constructs Volume One – A Theory of Personality.* Routledge, London. (originally published 1955 Norton, New York).

Kelly, G.A., (1991) *The Psychology of Personal Constructs. Volume Two – Clinical Diagnosis and Psychotherapy.* Routledge, London. (originally published 1955 Norton, New York).

Kelly, M.J. & O' Connor, B., (eds.) (1997) *Media Audiences in Ireland: Power and Cultural Identity.* University College Dublin Press, Ireland.

Kibert, D., (ed.) (1997) *Media in Ireland: The Search for Diversity* Open Air, Dublin.

Klein, R., (1994:) 'Anxiety disorders', in Rutter, M, Taylor E & Hersov, L (eds.) *Child and Adolescent Psychiatry: Modern Approaches,* 351-374.

Kobasa, S.C., (1979) 'Stressful life events, personality and health: An inquiry into hardiness', *Journal of Personality and Social psychology* 37, 1-11.

Kolb, B., & Whishaw, I.Q., (1996) *Fundamentals of Human Neuropsychology.* W.H. Freeman and Company, USA.

Kroger, J., (1996) *Identity in Adolescence: The Balance between Self and Other.* Routledge, London. [second edition]. Adolescence and Society Series.

Laufer, M., (ed.)(1995) *The Suicidal Adolescent.* Karnac Books, London.

Laurent, J., & Stark, K. D., (1993) 'Testing the cognitive contentspecificity hypothesis with anxious and depressed youngsters'. *Journal of Abnormal Psychology*, 102, 226-237.

Lawlor, M., & James, D., (2000) 'Prevalence of psychological problems in Irish school going adolescents', *Irish Journal of Psychological Medicine* 17(4): 117-122

Lazarus, R.S. & Folkman, S., (1984) *Stress appraisal and coping.* Springer, New York.

Lees, S., (1994) *Sugar and Spice: Sexuality and Adolescent Girls.* Penguin, London.

Levinsohn, P.M., Roberts, R.E., Seeley, J.R., Rohde, P., Gotlib, I.H., Hops, H., (1994) 'Adolescent Psychopathology: II Psychosocial Risk Factors for Depression', *Journal of Abnormal Psychology* 103, 302-315.

Lezak. M.D., (1983) *Neuropsychological Assessment.* Oxford University Press, Oxford [second edition].

Lynch, F., Mills, C., Daly, I., & Fitzpatrick, C., (2002) 'Challenging Time: coping with life stress in childhood and adolescence'. Presentation to The Royal College of Psychiatrists Residential Child Psychiatry Conference, Harrogate. September 2002.

Lynch, K., (1987) 'Dominant ideologies in Irish educational thought', *Economic and Social Review,* 18, 2. 110-122.

Lynch, K., (1988) 'Streaming and banding in schools: context and implications', *Journal of the Institute of Guidance Counsellors,* 14.

Lynch, K (1989) *The Hidden Curriculum.* Falmer, Lewes.

Mac Gréil, M., (1996) *Prejudice In Ireland Revisited.* Survey and Research Unit, St Patrick's College, Maynooth.

Macmann, G.M., & Barnett, D.W., (1994) 'Some Additional Lessons from the Wechsler Scales: A Rejoinder to Kaufman and Keith', *School Psychology Quarterly* Vol. 9. No. 3. 223-236.

Maguire, K. & Byrne, T., (2001:279-287) 'You Can Make a Difference: The Problem of Suicide', in Foster-Ryan, S. & Monahan, L. (eds.) (2001) *Echoes of Suicide,* Veritas, Dublin.

Martin, M., Williams, R. M., & Clark, D. M., (1991) 'Does anxiety lead to selective processing of threat-related information?' *Behaviour Research and Therapy,* 29, 147-160.

McClure, G. M.G., (2001) 'Suicide in Children and Adolescents in England and Wales 1970-1998', *British Journal of Psychiatry* 178, 469-474.

McCormack, W., (1998) *Lost for Words: Dyslexia at Second Level and Beyond.* Tower Press, Dublin.

McGuinness, C., (1993) 'Teaching Thinking: New signs for theories of cognition', *Educational Psychology* 13, 305-316.

McGuinness, C., (1996) 'Teaching thinking: Learning to think – thinking to learn', *The Irish Journal of Psychology* 17, 1 1-12.

McNamee, S. Gergen, K.J., (eds.) (1992) *Therapy As Social Construction.* Sage Publications, London.

McPhillips, M., Harper, P.G., Mulhern, G., (2000) 'Effects of replicating primary reflex movements on specific reading difficulties in children', *Lancet,* 355, 5, 33-41.

McPhillips, M., (2001) 'The role of persistent primary reflexes in reading delay', *Dyslexia Review* 13, 1 4-7.

Meredeen, S., (1988) *Study for Survival and Success. Guidenotes for College Students.* (PCP) Paul Chapman Publishing Ltd., Scotland.

Miles, M.B., & Huberman, A.M., (1994) *Qualitative Data Analysis.* Sage, London.

Moffit, T.E., (1993) 'The Neuropsychology of Conduct Disorder', *Developmental Psychopathology,* 1993, 5, 135-151.

Mogg, K., Bradley, B. P., Williams, R., & Mathews, A., (1993) 'Subliminal processing of emotional information in anxiety and depression', *Journal of Abnormal Psychology,* 102, 304-311.

Monahan, L., (2001) 'Bereavement and Tragedy: Learnings For the School', in Foster-Ryan, S & Monahan, L (eds.) *Echoes of Suicide,* Veritas, Dublin.

Moran, A.P., (1990) 'Allegiance to the Work Ethic, Achievement Motivation and Fatalism in Irish and American people', *Irish Journal of Psychology,* 11, 1, 82-96.

Moran, A.P., (1994) 'Coping with Pressure: Some Lessons from Sport Psychology', in Keane, C., (ed.) *Nervous Breakdown*. RTÉ/Mercier Press, Cork. 195-219.

Moran, A.P., (1997) *Managing your Own Learning at University: A Practical Guide*. University College Dublin Press, Dublin.

Morgan, M., Flanagan, R., Kellaghan, T., (2001) *A Study of Non-Completion in Undergraduate University Courses,* Dublin HEA.

Mulcahy, D., & O'Sullivan, D., (1989) *Educational Policy: Process and Substance*. Institute of Public Administration, Dublin.

Murray, M., (1994) 'Sleep Problems', in Keane, C., (ed.) *Nervous Breakdown*. RTÉ/Mercier Press, Cork.

Murray, M., (1995) 'What are our children watching?' *ASTIR Journal of the Association of Secondary Teachers Ireland,* Vol XXV No. 3.

Murray, M., (1997) 'Adolescence', in Keane, C., (ed.) *Nervous Breakdown*. RTÉ/Mercier Press, Cork.

Murray, M., (1997b) 'Dancing on The Edge with Adolescents: The co-construction of identity using the film medium in adolescent therapy', *Proceedings of Fifth European Congress of Psychology,* Dublin, Ireland.

Murray, M., & Keane, C., (1997) *The Teenage Years*. RTÉ/Mercier Press, Cork.

Murray, M., & Keane, C., (1998) *The ABC of Bullying*. RTÉ/Mercier Press, Cork.

Murray M., (1999a) 'Tele-Therapy: A new systemic approach to using film in adolescent psychotherapy', Peking University, Beijing, China.

Murray, M., (1999b:46) 'Tele-Therapy. The Use of Film in An Anti-Bullying Therapy with Children and Adolescents', *Proceedings of 1st International Conference on Promoting Mental Health at School*, Helsinki, Finland.

Murray, M., (2000) *On your Marks*. RTÉ Radio One. Six-Part Series on Preparation for Junior and Leaving Cert. Examinations. Series Producer: Peter Mooney. Series Presenter: Mary Kennedy.

Murray, M., (2000a) 'Leaving nothing to chance: Advice to Leaving Cert. Students and their Parents.' *Sunday Tribune*, 30 April 2000.

Murray, M., (2001a) 'Tele-Therapy: Adolescent Psychotherapy and Film', *Proceedings of The International Psychotherapy Group*. Beijing, China.

Murray, M., (2001b) 'Parenting Adolescents', *Working Notes* 39, 15-19.

Northedge, A., (1990) *The Good Study Guide*. The Open University Press, Milton Keynes.

O'Connor, R. & Sheehy, N., (2000) *Understanding Suicidal Behaviour.* BPS Books, Leicester.

O'Hanlon, B., (1998) *Stress: The Common Sense Approach.* Newleaf, Gill and Macmillan, Dublin.

Oltmanns, T.F., & Emery, R.E., (1995) *Abnormal Psychology.* Prentice Hall, New Jersey, USA.

O'Sullivan, M., & Fitzgerald, M (1988) 'Suicidal Ideation and acts of self-harm among Dublin school children', *Journal of Adolescence* 21: 427-433.

Parry-Jones, W.L (1985) 'Adolescent Disturbance', in Rutter, M. & Hersov, L., (eds.) *Child and Adolescent Psychiatry: Modern Approaches*. Blackwell Scientific Publications, Oxford. 584-598.

Piaget, J (1972) 'Intellectual evolution from adolescence to adulthood', *Human Development* 5, 1-12.

Piaget J, & Inhelder, B., (1958) *The Growth of Logical Thinking from Childhood to Adolescence*. Routledge and Kegan Paul, London.

Potter, J., (1996) *Representing Reality: Discourse, Rhetoric and Social Construction.* Sage, London.

Raskin, P.M., (1994) 'Identity and career counselling of adolescents: the development of a vocational identity', in Archer, S.L (ed.) *Interventions for Adolescents' Identity Development,* Sage, Newbury Park CA.

Renouf, A.G., & Harter, S., (1990) 'Low Self-Worth and Anger as Components of the Depressive Experience in Young Adolescents', *Development and Psychopathology,* 2, 293-310.

Reville, J. (1996) *Yes You Can: A Student's Guide to Study, Revision and Exam Success.* Folens, Dublin.

Rickson, B., (1998) 'The Relationship between undergraduate student counselling and successful degree completion', *Studies in Higher Education,* 23, 1 95-103.

Rickson, B. & Turner J., (2002) 'A Model for Supportive Services in Higher Education', in Stanley, N. & Manthorpe, J., (eds.) *Student's Mental Health Needs: Problems and Responses.* Jessica Kingsley Publishers, London. 171-192.

Rowley, J., Ganter, K., & Fitzpatrick, C., (2001) 'Suicidal thoughts and acts in Irish adolescents. *Irish Journal of Psychological Medicine,* 18, 82 -86.

Rutter, M., Tizard, J., Yule, W., Graham, P., & Whitmore, K., (1976) Isle of Wight Studies 1964-1974', *Psychological Medicine:* 6 313-332.

Rutter, M. Graham, P. Chadwick, O.F.D & Yule, W., (1976) 'Adolescent turmoil: fact or fiction?' *Journal of Child Psychology and Psychiatry* 17, 35-56.

Rutter, M, Maughan, P., Mortimer, P., Ouston, J., & Smith. A., (1979) *Fifteen Thousand Hours; Secondary Schools and their effects on Children.* Open Books, London.

Rutter, M. & Hersov, L., (eds.) (1985) *Child and Adolescent Psychiatry: Modern Approaches.* Blackwell Scientific Publications, Oxford.

Ryan, M., (2001) 'Suicide Prevention in Schools', in Foster-Ryan, S & Monahan, L (eds.) *Echoes of Suicide,* Veritas, Dublin. 182-200.

Sarnthein, J., vonStein, A., Rappelsberger, P., Petsche, H., Rauscher, F.H., Shaw, G.L., (1997) 'Persistent patterns of braining activity on EEG coherence of study of the positive effect of music on spatial-temporal reasoning.' *Neurological Research,* 19: 107-116.

Schmolch, H., Squire, L., (2001) *Neuropsychology,* Vol. 15 (i) 30-38.

Schrijvers, J., (1991) 'Dialectics of a Dialogical Ideal: Studying Down, Studying Sideways and Studying Up.', in Nencel, L., & Pels, P., (eds.) (1991) *Constructing Knowledge; Authority and Critique in Social Science.* Sage, London. 162-179.

Schweitzer, R.D., Seth-Smith, M., & Callan, V., (1992) 'The relationship between self-esteem and psychological adjustment in young adolescents', *Journal of Adolescence* 15. 83-97.

Sharry, J., (2001) *Bringing up Responsible Teenagers,* Veritas, Dublin.

Sharry, J., Reid, P., & Donohoe, E., (2001) *When Parents Separate: Helping your children cope.* Veritas, Dublin.

Shaywitz, S.E. & Shaywitz, B.A., Pugh, K.R., Fulbright, R.K., (1998) 'Functional disruption in the organisation of the brain for reading in dyslexia', *Neurobiology* 95 5. 263-264.

Shaywitz, B.A., Shaywitz, S.E., Pugh, K.R., Mencl, W.E., Fulbright, R.K. Skudlarski, P., Constable, R.T., Marchione, K.E., Fletcher, J.M., Lyon, G.R., Gore, J.C., (2002) 'Disruption of posterior brain systems for reading in children with developmental dyslexia', *Biological Psychiatry* 52, 2 101-110.

Shotter, J., (1993) *Conversational Realities: Constructing Life through Language,* Sage, London.

Simmons, R.G., (1987) 'Self-esteem in Adolescence', in Honess, T. & Yardley, K., (eds.) (1987) *Self and Identity: Perspectives across the Lifespan.* Routledge & Kegan Paul, London. 172-192.

Smith, J.A., Harré, R. & Van Langenhove, L., (eds.) (1995) *Rethinking Methods in Psychology.* Sage. London.

Stanley, N. & Manthorpe, J., (2001) 'Responding to students' mental health needs: impermeable systems and diverse users', *Journal of Mental Health,* 10 41-52.

Stanley, N. & Manthorpe, J., (eds.) (2002) *Student's Mental Health Needs: Problems and Responses.* Jessica Kingsley Publishers, London.

Stanley, N. & Manthorpe, J., (2002:) 'Responding to Student Suicide', in Stanley, N. & Manthorpe, J., (eds.) *Student's Mental Health Needs: Problems and Responses.* Jessica Kingsley Publishers, London. 243-260.

Steinberg, D., (1986) 'Psychiatric aspects of problem behaviour in schools: a consultative approach', in Tattum, D., (ed.) *Management of Disruptive Behaviour in Schools.* John Wiley and Sons, Chichester. 187-205.

Steinberg, D., (1987) *Basic Adolescent Psychiatry.* Blackwell Scientific Publications, London.

Sternberg, R.J., (1993) 'Procedures for identifying Intellectual Potential in the Gifted: A Perspective on Alternative "Metaphors of Mind"', in Heller, K.A., Monks, F.J. & Passow, A.H., (eds) *International Handbook of Research and Development of Giftedness and Talent.* Pergamon Press, England.

Tattum, D., (ed.) (1986) *Management of Disruptive Behaviour in School.* John Wiley and Sons, Chichester.

Tedlow, J.R., Fava, M. Uebelacker, LA Alpert, J.E., Nierenberg, A.A. & Rosenbaum, J. F., (1996) 'Are Study Dropouts

Different From Completers?', *Biological Psychiatry* 40, 7 668-671.

Terman M., Terman, J.S. Quitkin, F.M. et al (1989) 'Light therapy for seasonal affective disorder: A review of efficacy', *Neuropsychopharmacology* 2, 1-22.

Thomas, E.L., & Robinson, H.A., (1982) *Improving Reading in Every Class*. Allyn and Bacon, Boston.

Thompson P.M., Giedd J.N., Woods R.P., et al. 'Growth patterns in the developing brain detected by using continuum mechanical tensor maps', *Nature*, 2000; 404(6774): 190-3.

Tompkins, C.A., & Mateer, C.A., (1985) 'Right Hemisphere appreciation of intonational and linguistic indications of affect', *Brain and Language* 1985 24. 185-203.

Vygotsky, L.S. (1986) *Thought and Language,* MIT Press Cambridge MA (Originally published 1934).

Townsend, S., (1985) *The Growing Pains of Adrian Mole*. Methuen, London.

Wallerstein, J. S (1991) 'The Long-Term Effects of Divorce on Children – A Review', *Journal of American Academy of Child and Adolescent Psychiatry*. 30 349-360.

Warner, M.H., Ernst, J., Townes, B.D., Peel, J., & Preston, M., (1987) 'Relationship between IQ and neuropsychological measures in neuropsychiatric populations: Within laboratory and cross-cultural replications using WAIS and WAIS-R', *Journal of Clinical and Experimental neuropsychology*, 9 545-562.

Watkins, M.W., & Kush, J.C., (1994) 'Wechsler Subtest Analysis: The Right Way, The Wrong Way, or No Way?', *School Psychology Review,* 1994 Vol.23, No. 4. 640-651.

Wechsler, D., (1992) *Manual for the Wechsler Intelligence Scale for Children – Third Edition UK Edition*. The Psychological Corporation, Sidcup, Kent.

Weinmann, L.L., & Newcombe, N., (1990) 'Relational Aspects of Identity: Late adolescents' perceptions of their relationships with parents', *Journal of Experimental Child Psychology* 50. 357-369.

Williams, H., Fitzgerald, M. & Kinsella, M., (1989) 'Psychological Distress and Attitude to Authority in a Sample of Irish adolescents', *Irish Journal of Psychological Medicine*, 6 37-40.

Willis, T. & Filer, M., (1996) 'Stress-coping model of adolescent substance use', in T. Ollendick & R. Prinz (eds.) *Advances in Clinical Child Psychology*, Oxford, New York. 501-530.

Wires, J.W., Barocas, R., & Hollenbeck, A.R., (1994) 'Determinants of adolescent identity development: a cross-sequential study of boarding school boys', *Adolescence* 29 361-378.

USEFUL INFORMATION

Information in a book can never replace direct, personal assessment and professional advice in any instance where you as parents or students are upset, worried, unsure or concerned. There are many situations described in this book where such professional help is indicated or advised and do please follow the well-tried dictum, 'when in doubt check it out'. It is always preferable to err on the side of caution.

Your local GP or Health Board should be the first port of call if you are uncertain about what specific referral may be required. For your convenience the contact details for the Health Boards are listed below.

In most instances your GP will refer you directly to the appropriate organisation or agency. Additionally, GPs will probably be acquainted with local support groups and centres, and community information or advice centres. Obviously, emergency numbers are in the telephone directly or available from Directory Inquiries. If you do not get through at once on a helpline number, keep trying as these lines can get quite busy.

On the following pages are the addresses and contact numbers of some useful organisations. Many of them have nationwide branches.

ACLD
*(The Association for
Children and Adults with
Learning Difficulties)*
Suffolk Chambers,
1 Suffolk Street,
Dublin 2
Tel: (01) 679 0276

*Al Anon (AA), Family
Groups*
5/6 Capel Street,
Dublin 1
Tel: 01 873 2699

Alateen
*[To help young people whose
lives have been upset by a
parent's compulsive drinking]*
5/6 Capel Street,
Dublin 1
Tel: 01 873 2699

*AWARE – Helping to Defeat
Depression*
72 Lower Leeson Street,
Dublin 2
Tel: (01) 676 6166

*CAO Central Applications
Office,*
Tower House,
Eglinton Street,
Galway
Tel: (091) 509800

*Department of Education
and Science (Special
Education Section)*
Cornamaddy
Athlone
Co. Westmeath
Tel: (0902) 74621
Web Address:
www.irlgov.ie

*Department of Education
and Science (General)*
Marlborough Street
Dublin 1
Tel: (01) 873-4700
Web address: www.irlgov.ie

*Family Therapy Association
of Ireland*
73 Quinn's Road
Shankill
Co. Dublin
Tel: (01) 2722105
Web Address: www.ifta-
familytherapy.org

Health Boards:

*East Coast Area Health
Board*
ECAHB Southern Cross
House,
Southern Cross Business
Park,
Boghall Road.
Bray, Co. Wicklow
Tel: (01) 2765682

South Western Health Board
Oak House,
Limetree Ave.,
Millenium Park,
Naas,
Co. Kildare
Tel: (045) 875772

Northern Area Health Board
Unit 2
Swords Business Campus,
Balheany Road,
Swords,
Co Dublin
Tel: (01) 8131800

Midland Health Board
Arden Road,
Tullamore,
Co. Offaly
Tel: (0506) 21868

Mid Western Health Board
31/33 Catherine Street,
Limerick,
Tel: (061) 316655

North Eastern Health Board
Kells, Co. Meath
Tel: (046) 40341

North Western Health Board
Enniskillen,
Manorhamilton,
Co. Leitrim
Tel: (072) 20400

South Eastern Health Board,
Lacken,
Dublin Road,
Kilkenny
Tel: (056) 20400

Southern Health Board
Dennehy's Cross,
Wilton,
Co. Cork
Tel: (021) 4545011

Western Health Board
Marlin Park,
Galway
Tel: (091) 751131

*Irish Association of Teachers
in Special Education*
Education Centre,
St. Patrick's College,
Drumcondra,
Dublin 9
Tel: (01) 837-6191
Fax: (01) 837-0642
E-mail:
info@iatseireland.com
Web Address:
www.iatseireland.com

*National Educational
Psychological Service*
Frederick Court
24/27 North Frederick
Street
Dublin
Tel: (01) 889-2700
Fax: (01) 889-2755
Web Address:
oasis.gov.ie/education/pri
mary_education/national_
educational_psychological
_service.html

*National Parent's Council –
Secondary*
Marion Institute of
Education
Griffith Avenue
Dublin 9
Tel: (01) 857-0522
Web Address:
www.edunet.ie/parents

*Parentline
(Organisation for parents
under stress)*
Carmichael House,
North Brunswick Street,
Dublin 7
Tel (01) 873 3500

*Post-Leaving Certificate
Courses (PLC) / Youthreach,*
Marlborough Street,
Dublin 1
Tel: (01) 8892015

*Psychological Society of
Ireland*
2a Corn Exchange Place
Dublin 2
Tel: (01) 671-7122
Web address:
www.psy.it/ordpsic/psy_e_
u/psi_cx.html

*Rainbows
(Facilitates groups to help
children, teenagers, young
adults and parents who have
suffered loss through death,
separation or divorce)*
Rainbows National Office,
Loreto Centre,
Crumlin Road,
Dublin 12
Tel / Fax: (01) 473 4175

*Samaritans
(Befriends the lonely and
despairing)*
112 Marlborough Street,
Dublin 1
Tel: (01) 872 7700
See your local telephone
directory for branches in
your area.

*Sólás (Barnardos)
Bereavement Counselling for
Children*
18 St Patrick's Hill,
Cork

Also Christchurch Square,
Dublin 8
Tel: (01) 473 2110

*Steps Youth Advice and
Counselling Service*
30/31 Bride Street,
Dublin 2
Tel: (01) 473 4143
or
40 Abbey Street,
Wexford
(053) 238646
or
12 Mary Street,
Cork
Tel: (021) 496 2949
or
22 Thomas Street,
Limerick
Tel: (061) 400 088
or
37 Georges Street,
Waterford
Tel: (051) 304476

*UCAS University and
College Admissions Service,*
Fulton House,
Jessop Avenue,
Cheltenham,
Gloucestershire,
GLE 503 35H
England